FLEXIBLE COMPOSITE MATERIALS

IN ARCHITECTURE, CONSTRUCTION AND INTERIORS

René Motro (Ed.)

FLEXIBLE COMPOSITE MATERIALS

IN ARCHITECTURE, CONSTRUCTION AND INTERIORS

BIRKHÄUSER
BASEL

This publication was made possible by the
kind support of Serge Ferrari Group.

Layout and cover design: PROXI, Barcelona

Project management:
Henriette Mueller-Stahl, Berlin

Copy editing: Richard Palmer,
Divonne-les-Bains

Translation of the following contributions
from French: ARCHITEXT (Anne Kuhn,
Jürgen Hübner, Derek Henderson) Dresden
and Marseille
*Flexible Composite Materials: production and
modern uses of a polymorphic material* by
Jean Vasseur
Design details for successful implementation
by Bernard Doriez and René Motro

This book does not make reference to existing
patents, registered designs, trade marks, etc.
If such reference has been omitted, this does
not signify that the product or the product
name is not protected. The great number of
different materials and products mentioned
in this book made it impossible to carry an
investigation into the possible existence of
trademark protection in every case.
Accordingly, in the interest of uniformity,
the text makes no use of trademark symbols
such as ® or TM.

Authors of case studies:
Richard Palmer: rp
Arno Pronk: ap
Wolfgang Sterz: ws
Jean Vasseur: jv
Ivo Vrouwe: iv

This book is also available in a German
language edition (ISBN 978-3-7643-8971-0)
and a French language edition (ISBN 978-3-
0346-0709-4).

A CIP catalogue record for this book is available from the Library of Congress, Washing-
ton D.C., USA

Bibliographic information published by the
German National Library
The German National Library lists this publi-
cation in the Deutsche Nationalbibliografie;
detailed bibliographic data are available on
the Internet at http://dnb.d-nb.de.
© 2013 Birkhäuser Verlag GmbH,
Basel
P.O. Box 44, 4009 Basel, Switzerland
Part of De Gruyter

Printed on acid-free paper produced from
chlorine-free pulp. TCF ∞

Printed in Germany

ISBN 978-3-7643-8972-7

9 8 7 6 5 4 3 2 1

www.birkhauser.com

CASE STUDIES

by INES DE GIULI
and ROMAIN FERRARI

FLEXIBLE COMPOSITE MATERIALS: PRODUCTION AND MODERN USES OF A POLYMORPHIC MATERIAL

One of technical textile's many forms.

INTRODUCTION

Textile – coming from the Latin word *textilis*, derived from the verb *texere* which means, "to weave or warp a cloth or a woof, to plait or to interlace" – appeared very early in the history of humanity. Archaeologists have discovered pieces of fabric dating back to at least 8000 years BC. They were found in Mesopotamia where flax was grown. In Egypt, the country also known as "the land of flax", there are some fabric relics that were produced around 4500 BC. It was certainly a time when textiles were uniquely made of natural fibres. Today they are characterised by a large and ever increasing variety of types and uses.

Technological advances have not only allowed the development of new generations of fibres – synthetic, in addition to natural – but also of new manufacturing processes, which multiply the properties and lead to a diversification of application fields.

Whilst initially, and for a long period, used almost exclusively for clothing, today's textiles are present in aeronautics, electronics, medicine and construction. They are the object of constant innovation, which seeks to adapt them to meet increasing demands from newly discovered fields. By integrating the concepts of durability and energy efficiency, the textile industry has proven that it can tackle these issues that confront all main industrial sectors today. Thanks to university networks and institutions, research centres and laboratories, multidisciplinary expertise is used to create new generations of highly specialised products. As shown by the historical evidence of several thousand years of civilisation, textiles continue to evolve with the challenges faced by our modern society.

TEXTILE: A POLYMORPHIC MATERIAL

TRADITIONAL TEXTILES

Textiles today cover an extremely wide field of materials. While defined by the manufacturing process, the weave (as the etymology of the word "textile" itself suggests), a large part of its properties come from the principal material with which it is fabricated: the fibre. Moreover it is very often and significantly the textile's fibre itself, such as "linen", "silk" or "cotton", which gives the name to the final product. The first distinction that is made when seeking to categorise textiles is both modern, since it draws upon history, and related to the manufacture of the material; this is the distinction between a traditional, and a technical textile. The former, whose manufacture and use are the oldest, is associated with concerns of appearance and comfort, and thus covers clothing and also furniture; from bed sheets to tapestry, from tablecloths to draperies. By contrast, a technical textile can be defined as any other textile, where the technical features and functional properties prevail over the esthetical and decorative characteristics. This category, however, appears less a separate industrial branch than an extension and diversification of the traditional textile industry. The distinction comes from the intensive development of the industry at the beginning of the last century, following scientific progress and the emergence of new generations of fibres derived from chemical processes.

Above: Extrusion process.   Below: Weaving process.

THE TEXTILE IN TECHNICAL APPLICATIONS
(TTA, TECHNICAL TEXTILES)

From the 1980s the Western European textile industry suffered constant decline, resulting mainly from the strong competition of low-wage countries such as China or several Eastern European countries. This heightened competition led to the loss of thousands of jobs and to the closing of numerous factories in what was once a key European business sector. A lot of manufacturers traditionally involved in the clothing industry are endeavouring to move into high value-added markets, less affected by labour costs and offering better profit margins. Today new technical fibres represent an increasingly large part of the textile markets in Europe, notably in Germany, France and Italy, but also in the USA and Japan. In the move, already well underway, toward functional textiles for technical applications, the new constraints are the physical, mechanical and chemical performance requirements. Manufacturers of state-of-the-art textiles today employ the most modern production processes, fulfilling extremely precise specifications and including rigorous quality control. The manufacture of technical textiles involves four major steps. The first step concerns forming the yarn using an assembly of filaments that vary in number from one to several hundred; usually they are obtained by the extrusion of melted polyester granules or glass beads. The heated material is introduced and pushed through a spinneret (a metal piece serving as a mould), which gives it an elongated form before being stretched. The second step, the weaving of the yarn, gives birth to the actual fabric, at this stage still termed "raw", as it has not been bleached or otherwise treated. The third step consists of applying a "conditioner" to the raw fabric, usually of a PVC, silicone or PTFE base, enriched with chemical components such as dye, softeners, thermal stabilisers, antifungal agents or others. This coating may be applied to one or both sides of the fabric, a process that may be repeated several times. The application of a surface varnish, the fourth step, completes the manufacture of the textile, for which one final step remains: packaging in the form of bolts.

In the case of coated textiles, the raw fabric undergoes a certain number of pre-treatments before being coated on one or both sides, as mentioned, with PVC (polyvinyl chloride), with silicone in the case of polyester fabrics, or with PTFE (polytetrafluoroethylene). The varnish itself usually consists of a fluoridated lacquer that waterproofs the surface, in the manner of polyester fabrics coated with PVC, in order to make them more resistant against stains, mould and ultra-violet rays.
It is the combination of different functions that define the technical character of the textile. Thus the final product has qualities variously adapted to the intended use: a weight, or grammage, ranging between 250 and 1500 g/m², a thickness varying from 0.5 to 1.5 mm, a width measured in centimetres, a breaking strength in traction and tearing resistance between 150 and 1500 daN/5 cm (in other words the rupture of a 5 cm band occurs at a traction that corresponds to a load ranging from 150 to 1500 daN according to the fabric). The range of qualities may also include: stretching under static load, a greater or lesser porosity, fire-resistance (some textiles are even rated non-combustible), a resistance to micro-organisms, plus other mechanical resistances such as abrasion. Textiles can be produced with colours that withstand heat, humidity and ultraviolet rays, that are either able to transmit or to reflect light, even solar energy, or that exhibit certain acoustic and thermal properties (very thin materials can absorb up to 60% of acoustical waves – textiles for blinds can block 70% to 96% of solar heat).

Above: Weaving factory set-up.   Below: Final flexible composite.

TEXTILE TECHNOLOGY USED IN ARCHITECTURE

Three types of membrane make up 90% of those used in modern architectural designs: glass fibre – a composite material reinforced by glass filaments usually associated with polymers – coated with PTFE, PVC-coated polyester, and ETFE (Ethylene-Tetrafluoroethylene) sheet. Glass fibre coated with PTFE (Teflon), is the material that has been most used for pneumatic structures. Coated fabrics require practically no maintenance and are quite easy to replace. PTFE has only been used in buildings since the 1970s, while transparent high-performance ETFE sheet became established in the middle of the 1990s. Today PTFE-coated glass fibre is much more expensive. It is less elastic and has a low degree of flexibility, making it more susceptible to crazing and auto-abrasion of the coating.

Apart from these three principal membrane materials there exist, as mentioned by Philip Drew in his publication New Tent Architecture (New York: Thames & Hudson, 2008), many others: non-coated, perforated and micro-perforated membranes with good sound absorption capacity, non-coated or impregnated textiles with a looser or denser weave for indoor uses, polyester fabrics with inner coating for low flammability, low emissivity glass fabrics with fluoridated polymer coating and a structure that absorbs noise. According to Drew, the fabrics used in architecture constitute a highly specialised field.

Researchers continue to create new, more robust, and more resistant fibre materials. Consequently architectural textiles today can serve as filters to remedy undesired environmental effects such as direct sunlight. They can also produce electricity thanks to the integration of thin photovoltaic panels. In 2005 when Royal Philips Electronics presented textiles with integrated luminous diodes and without compromising the material's softness, the company gave birth to the photonic textile.

In the construction industry, textile and polymer technology is even now weaving its way into concrete structures. Fibres help to improve concrete's fire resistance by channelling steam to the surface, thereby preventing the explosive spalling that results from rapid intense heating. Polymers may be applied to coat metal reinforcement, and fibres can increase concrete's impermeability, two factors which effectively reduce the concrete thickness normally required for reinforcement corrosion protection, which in turn leads to lighter more efficient structures and savings in construction costs. Fibres can be added to concrete as reinforcement against cracking, allowing the conventionally used steel mesh reinforcement to be omitted. There are even treated fibres that, when added to the mix, enable concrete to conduct electricity.

Unlike traditional textiles, a sector showing little dynamism in Europe, technical fabrics are a rapidly expanding field. However their development requires expertise in new technologies that allow further cost reductions such as automation, and the improved reliability of both components and processes. The future of TTA not only depends on improving the flexibility of the manufacturing system, but also on the creation of products with very high added value such as intelligent fibres, also called *smart fibres*; these are interactive or adaptive products, namely textiles with information "sensors" and fibres that react to specific information. The manufacture of materials used in textiles for technical applications depends on research and processes that far exceed the simple assembly of yarns, in itself the result of a very specific experimental protocol.

MATERIAL PRODUCTION

PRODUCING THE YARN

Technical textile fibres are, per se, functional products with specific properties determined by their intended use. They can be woven, knitted or plaited, but also exist in a non-woven form. The resultant material normally has to undergo additional treatments before becoming a finished or half-finished product.

The fibres are obtained by extrusion of a chemical preparation, a procedure that offers the possibility of incorporating additives to change the material's properties according to the desired requirements. Continuous yarns are made of only a handful to several thousand fibres, with a diameter less than a micron in the case of microfibres or nanofibres, or about a millimetre in the case of monofilaments. Afterwards the spinning process allows fibres possessing different properties to be combined, e.g. aramid with pre-oxidised fibres for the production of hybrid yarns. The latter can be enriched by means of various modifications with the aim of giving the yarns new properties, either by coating, impregnation or adhesion of resins. Finally comes the sheathing process, which designates the wrapping of a core of usually elastomer yarns, e.g. made of elastane, by other yarns made of polyamide, polyester or cotton, or the twisting process, which can provide new mechanical properties.

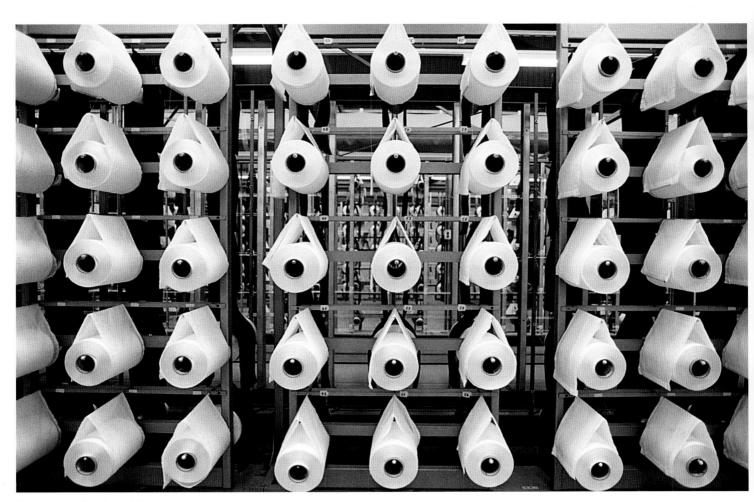

An array of textile bolts awaiting post treatment.

FROM YARN TO TEXTILE

The actual fabric production, the weaving, results from the interlacing of yarns that are placed in the direction of the fabric length (warp) by yarns that follow the direction of the fabric width (weft). Three fundamental types are distinguished in the traditional textile business: *plain weave*, obtained by lifting alternately the even or the uneven yarns of the warp to give way to the weft yarn, *twill weave* characterised by the presence of diagonal ribs on the front and flat ribs on the reverse side, and *satin weave*, fine and lustrous on the front and matt on the reverse side, thus forming the richest fabric from an arithmetical point of view. Indeed weaving offers an infinite variety of surfaces, from cloths with a unidirectional nap, to open weave fabric with only a few threads per square metre, or very heavy fabrics of several kilograms per square metre. Their properties essentially depend on the direction of the yarns or on the fibres with which they are made. One can create textile or fabric surfaces where the constituent yarns are woven to create a flat surface, or voluminous 3D textiles, where the yarns occupy three dimensions. In each category the orientation of the yarns on the flat surface can be axial, biaxial or multiaxial.

REFINING THE TEXTILES: SHAPING THE MATERIAL

Refining techniques have the objective of modifying the properties of raw textiles to provide them with specific characteristics, and to ensure they meet the functional requirements of the intended application. The textiles are first prepared according to various procedures such as, in traditional manufacturing, *buckling* to eliminate fibres sticking out of the fabric, *desizing* with the aim of removing previously applied components from the warp, and finally, thermal fixation to ensure the structural stability of the fabric. After preparation, the main refining operations are usually dyeing, printing or flocking, the latter being a spray procedure that produces a coating with a fibrous, velvety or fluffy surface. The use of chemical and mechanical finishing is also common, such as *emerizing*, which describes the softening of a fabric by putting it on a fast turning cylinder, also known as grinding. *Sizing*, a treatment specific to glass fabrics, is intended to make them compatible with resins to be later applied. To make a textile flameproof, hydrophobic, antistatic, antibacterial, anti-abrasive or uv-resistant, chemical finishes in the form of polymer resins are applied by coating. For this process the textile is immersed in a bath. There must be a high degree of compatibility between the fibre and the different formulations of polyvinyl chloride, polyurethane, acrylic, natural and synthetic elastomers that comprise the fabric treatment. Adherence requires, for example, the creation of chemical links between the macromolecules of a textile using a treatment called "Resorcine Formol Latex" that fixes a rubber-reactive component to the fibres. The adding of softeners, mineral substances or other additives further modifies the textile's properties, as required for its intended use. The resulting product may undergo additional treatment during which films, foams or microporous membranes made of polyurethane or PTFE are made to adhere to the textile support by lamination, thus adding barrier functions (breathability, waterproofing) to the finished material. There are also pre-impregnated textiles made of fibres associated with thermo-hardening or thermo-plastic resins. The raw material is then processed: in solution, when molten, in powder form, by hydridisation or transfer. While undergoing thermal treatment the pre-impregnated material is shaped in a mould.

The hydrophobic lotus leaf surface ...

... and its textile homologue.

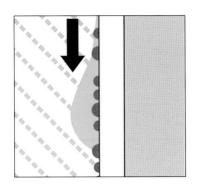

Conventional façade coating: the surface is less hydrophobic and thus more susceptible to wetting with water. Dirt particles adhere more easily.

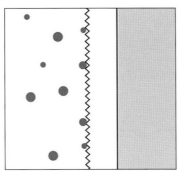

How the Lotus-Effect works in façade coating: the microtextured surface reduces the available contact area for dirt and water to a minimum.

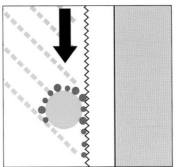

The surface is additionally ultra-hydrophobic. The rain drops roll off the surface immediately, taking the loosely deposited dirt particles with them.

The large diversity of materials and the very high complexity of manufacturing procedures require expertise and specific qualifications, especially in chemistry or mechanical physics, which underlines the importance of R&D in the textile sector. One of the great trends today is towards biomimetics, which takes inspiration from the functioning of living organisms.

NATURE: A LABORATORY FOR ADVANCING TEXTILE DEVELOPMENT?

Research into nanotechnologies is seen as of fundamental importance in technological innovation. Work is also focussing on the analysis of interesting biochemical behaviour found in the natural world. The challenge while observing such properties is to reproduce them artificially, an operation which has already led to some concrete results.

The lotus leaf has properties that have served as a model for dirt-repellent surfaces, also called self-cleaning surfaces. Its special nanometric structure traps air and makes the surface hydrophobic. Dirt cannot stick to it and any grime deposited on the surface is easily removed by rain. The company Sto has developed an external coating called Lotusan, based on the same microstructure principles, that uses rainwater to wash the surface clean. By reproducing the texture of the lotus leaf on a nanometric scale, it is possible to make a textile dirt-repellent. This can help to reduce the use of toxic detergents that until now have been used to clean surfaces exposed to the elements.

The fact that nature is a source of inspiration is accompanied by a parallel concern regarding the use of nature's resources. Beyond the accelerating technical advances of materials demanded by the requirements of the industrial sector and the necessity of technological innovation, the concept of sustainable development has begun to affect new textiles by placing restrictions on their composition. It has even become one of the priority goals of textile research centres in Europe, regardless of the area of application, resulting in larger investments for researching: recyclable properties, the biodegradability of fibres, decreasing waste in connection with chemical treatments, and energy reduction.

TEXTILES AS A CONTRIBUTION TO SUSTAINABLE CONSTRUCTION METHODS

Regarding architecture, Philip Drew admits that today the terms lightweight and renewable are the two key words of a responsible architecture from an ecological point of view. Sustainable development has become a major concern for all industrial sectors, and represents one of the main goals of textile research centres. Independent of the area of application, the range of sustainable products is characterised by two main tendencies related to the protection of the environment and a reduction in the use of energy. Research concentrates on the biodegradability of fibres, on the wish to limit the number of different materials used in one product, and on recyclability.

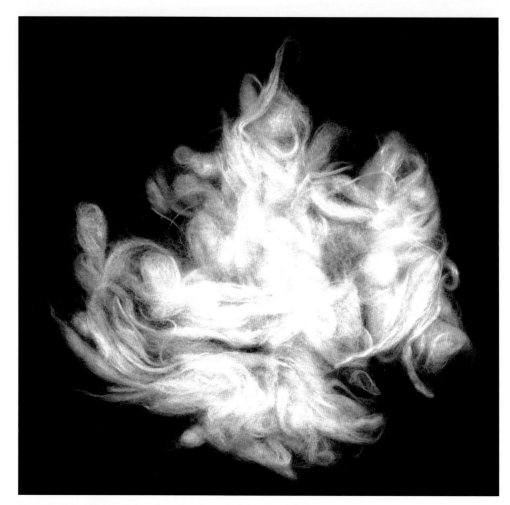

Above: Recycled fibres.   Below: Granules of recycled plasticised vinyl.

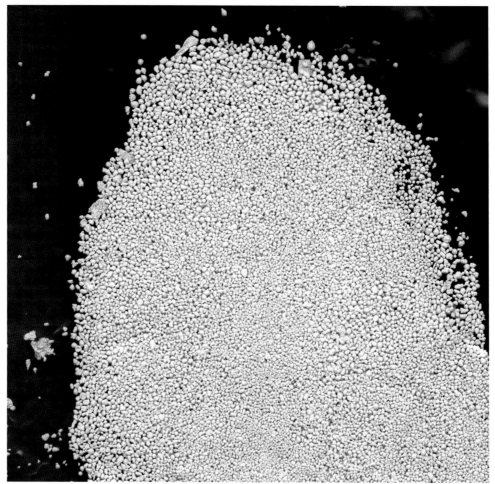

BIODEGRADABILITY AND
LIMITING THE USE OF CHEMICAL PRODUCTS

The use of natural fibres of plant origin is currently being explored to create new materials. New generations of disposable bags, but also surgical stents (tubes placed in arteries) have come on to the market. They are composed of polymers extracted from corn, such as polylactic acid (PLA).

Increasing attention is being paid to hemp, which can produce very good quality textiles and is recyclable. It is capable of providing efficient noise and thermal insulation, has non-flammable properties, strongly resists humidity, repels certain organisms and can store CO_2. For these reasons, in France for example, the plant has been included in the parliamentary bill on renewable biomaterials in the building sector, adopted by the French National Assembly in October 2008.

The development of polypropylene is a further example. It is easily recyclable and has attained high quality through advances in eco-design in the plastics industry.

Research into waste reduction in connection with the chemical treatment of fibres and textiles concerns moreover, all possible avenues. Great effort is being made to decrease the amount of pollution from this activity or to render the emitted waste more easily treatable. This translates, amongst other things, into incentives to limit the use of formalin, and to promote the adoption of new manufacturing technologies such as the development of gas processing for textiles, which limits the number of environmentally harmful chemical baths.

Other significant actions, such as the recovery and recycling of constituent elements of PVC, have been possible since 1998. The recycling of materials is one of the founding stages of sustainable construction.

RECYCLING

The central element of the sustainable development policy of the French company Serge Ferrari is the invention, development and application of a procedure – Texyloop – introduced in 2000, to allow the recycling of composite textiles. This procedure not only enables membranes to be recycled, it also aims to create new materials, which can then in part be reintroduced into the membrane fabrication process: thus the Texyloop cycle is created. The company opened an industrial recycling plant in Italy in 2002 and today more than 90% of its product range can be recycled. These recycled materials enter into the composition of a range of diverse products.

To promote this technology the company also took the initiative to create "Relais Textiles Techniques", the first European network for the collection of fabrics whose working life is exhausted, and of which it is a participating member. The network, operating since 2007, also encourages recycling initiatives established by other companies, such as Freitag in Switzerland and Reversible in France. The implementation of this systematic recycling loop involves a Lifecycle Analysis (LCA), a standardised method (ISO 14040-14043) consisting of a group of indicators that measure environmental impact. This provides information on all exploited resources; it measures the pollutants that are emitted during the production of a textile and makes it possible to determine the product's utilisation period, the method of its disposal and the recycling of its waste products.

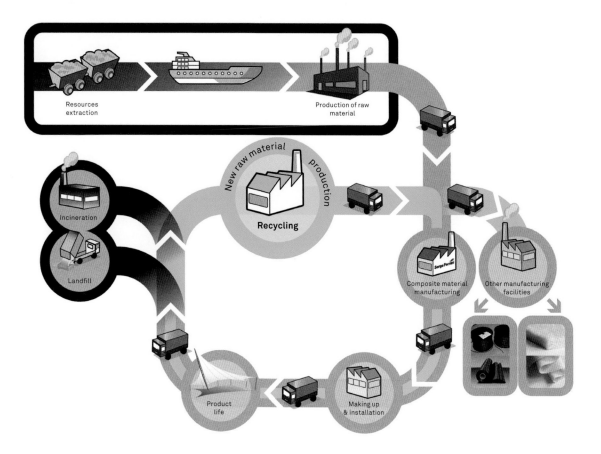

The LCAs, which are double-checked by independent international organisations such as the EVEA (France) and the CIRAIG (Canada), have systematically shown that the main environmental impact (on average 80%) is associated with the extraction and the production of raw materials. The recycling of products and the creation of new raw materials from this is therefore a decisive factor in significantly reducing the extent of environmental impact. The LCA established for the product Batyline gives clear evidence of the efficiency of the Texyloop initiative. It shows that recycling is extremely profitable in terms of limiting harmful effects and in contributing to sustainable development. Of course, the lifetime of materials also has a direct influence on energy savings.

THE CONCEPT OF SUSTAINABILITY

The sustainability of a product has to be considered in terms of its structural integrity and contractual guarantees, but also in terms of its aesthetic characteristics over the years. The long-term performance of the mechanical characteristics of a composite membrane is directly proportional to the thickness of the coating layer and the crest of the yarns. It is no longer the aim to produce very large quantities of disposable and renewable products, which will be buried, incinerated, dumped or burned in the open air at the end of their lifetime; the focus is rather on increasing the lifespan of the material, to make it modifiable and transformable. The Serge Ferrari group has also proved to be an innovator in this respect, especially with its range of Précontraint membranes which have a considerably extended lifetime due to an extremely efficient protective layer. During the coating process a fabric is normally kept under tension only in the direction of the warp. The Précontraint

Composite PVC membranes and textiles

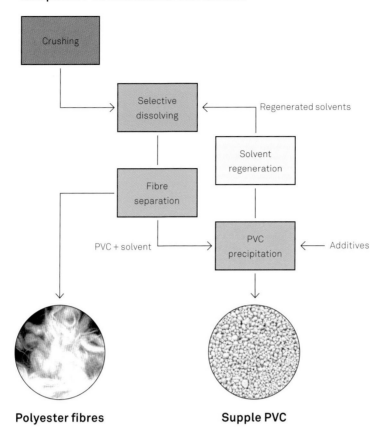

Polyester fibres   Supple PVC

technology, on the other hand, aims to keep the yarns of the fabric under tension in both directions, warp and weft. Holding it very flat at the moment of coating, the fabric attains an excellent level of protection of the yarns at both peaks and troughs of the surface profile, with a controlled thickness, a characteristic that has a direct impact on the weight. These performance enhancements facilitate the implementation of the textile in architecture, its deformations are easier to calculate, and they help improve the product's environmental quality, particularly concerning energy savings.

TEXTILES AS THEY CONTRIBUTE TO ENERGY SAVINGS

The particular properties of textiles integrated into buildings can also contribute to sustainable construction by influencing the total energy balance. The quality of certain textiles concerning transparency, translucence, insulation and solar protection are additional benefits for low energy buildings. At Serge Ferrari, the function (LowE) is obtained by the calibrated application of an aluminised treatment to the fabric. This acts as a thermal barrier: in winter the textile retains heat and in summer repels heat, helping to reduce climate control costs. This function reinforces the thermal solutions already afforded by flexible membranes used notably to provide permanent or removable solar protection to building façades. In addition, the fabric's translucence is not reduced, thereby not impeding the transmission of natural light.

The international exhibition in Shanghai in 2010 showed different examples of sustainable architecture based on the use of textiles. For instance, there was the "Bamboo House", presented by the Madrid Pavilion at the exhibition and accessed through the "Air Tree", a bioclimatic building designed by the Madrid architectural office Ecosistema Urbano, which uses wind and solar energies for its operation. The awnings, made of Serge Ferrari screens Soltis 86 and 92 fabric, tilt with the changing light intensity, thereby imitating a plant's phototropic response to its surrounding environment. When night falls, they retract to reveal a previously hidden "bark" of screens Soltis B92 endowed with insulating thermal characteristics and which can partially conceal the exterior, thus creating a new intermediate space. The translucent and luminous quality of the centre of the "tree" is created by an additional shell made of Serge Ferrari Précontraint 402 fabric. The roof is composed of an opaque Précontraint 702 S membrane with a motif imprint facing the sky, and on the reverse side a perforated screens Soltis 86 fabric, which offers a view of the motifs while screening visitors from the sun's rays.

The German pavilion tackled the problem of sustainable construction head on: with an image of dynamic town-planning, this pavilion reflected the diversity of life in the German cities and countryside. The four large exhibition buildings, intertwined with each other, provided a symbol of solidarity. Individually each structure would be in precarious equilibrium, by interacting they attain perfect harmony. This interdependence highlights the connections between the interior and exterior spaces, the play of light and shade, of building and nature, of urban and rural landscapes. Such equilibrium is a necessary environmental responsibility. The choice of Stamisol, an eco-designed, sustainable and 100% recyclable textile, as the textile for the façade, is a decisive element for the project's coherence.

Madrid Pavilion at EXPO Shanghai 2010.

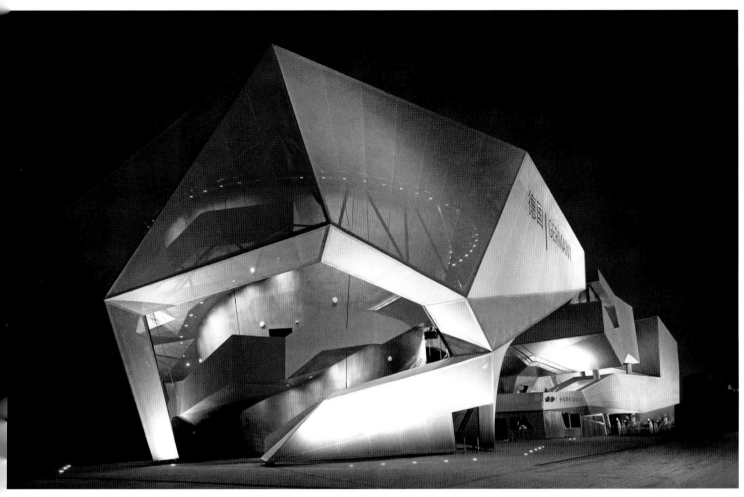

German Pavilion at EXPO Shanghai 2010.

CONCLUSION

Textiles underwent a revolution in the 20th century from purely domestic use, more or less widespread, towards industrial use, thus giving birth to a wide range of application. The subtle and complex ways of synthesising and manufacturing fibres has undoubtedly turned this into a high technology sector, to the point where textiles provide solutions in the most unexpected places. Just as they are increasingly becoming useful materials to civil engineers, alongside concrete or steel, the concerns of our time reinvest textiles with an essential ingredient: that of nature. Whether in imitation or respect, textile research closely observes our natural world and at the same time honours it. If we are to believe Philip Drew, who places textiles at the heart of the debate of modernity in architecture, and if we recognise the efforts of manufacturers to make this material the central element of a new urbanism, one that takes account of its environmental impact, then this material has every opportunity of seeing its identity evolve from being our second skin to being our building's second skin, at the same time protective *and* inspiring.

The "Tubaloon", a temporary stage for the musical festival in Kongsberg, Norway.

by BERNARD MAURIN
and RENÉ MOTRO

②

TEXTILE ARCHITECTURE

CONCEPTUAL DESIGN PROCESS

The basic idea for a textile architecture project originates during early meetings between the architect and the engineer. The morphologic richness of such projects is provided by the varying curvatures of shapes, in contrast to the classical straight lines of orthogonal architecture. However the rules of construction are quite different in terms of realisation and of mechanical behaviour: textile membranes are subjected to a pre-stress conferring them their rigidity, and a major objective is to manage the coupling between internal forces and curvatures for a given material. This explains the necessity of collaborative work between architects and engineers from the early stages of the conceptual design process, in order to offer the best morphological expression while ensuring the feasibility of the project.

The first drawings are progressively formalised by the architect so as to define the overall shape and the main components, such as principal masts (2.1).

2.1

Membrane in the style of a "double Chinese hat".
Standalone solution. First drawings and models.

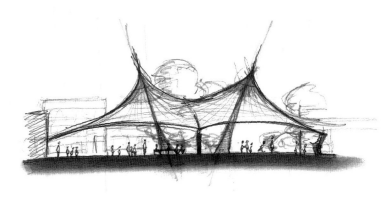

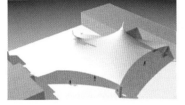

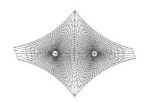 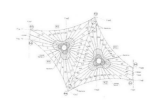

Form-finding process with dedicated software.

On the basis of these first drawings the engineer has to model the project, determining the shape using a so-called "form-finding process", based on numerical methods. Several commercial or proprietary software applications are available: all the fixed points have to be defined during this form-finding stage (2.2).

The sizing of the membrane is determined by a mechanical study under external loads that are defined by reference to current design rules. It must be underlined that climatic loads (wind and snow) are taken into account by combining their effects with those of the membrane pre-stress. A very important stage of the engineering study relies upon the so-called "cutting pattern": the designer has to geometrically define the flat strips that will, once assembled, constitute the curved surface. Many criteria are taken into account, aesthetics, durability, but also those related to the orthotropic character of the textile. Several methods are used in order to reach a shape in accordance with the initial morphology, not forgetting the importance of reducing the size of the strips. This size reduction facilitates the pre-stressing of the strips during assembly, in agreement with the level fixed during the mechanical behaviour calculations (2.3).

2.3

 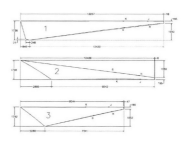

Cutting, welding and assembling the strips inside the factory.

The membrane can then be transported to the site, positioned, fixed to main masts and other anchoring points, before implementation of the calculated pre-stress allows the desired morphology to be realised (2.4).

2.4

Final realisation.

Cables and beam: tension T would be infinite for cables.

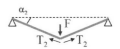

V-shape as elementary curved geometrical model.

BASIC ENGINEERING PRINCIPLES

Architectural textiles, when used for achieving shaped membranes, are under tension before the action of any external loads; this tension is known as initial pre-stress (also referred to as pretension). The overall membrane rigidity is further conditioned by its curvature at any point. Curvature and pre-stress are characteristic of membrane design. When compared to classical engineering studies, two specific main stages apply for membranes:

- the form-finding process enables the geometrical definition of their surfaces, which is closely coupled with the pre-stress distribution;
- the patterning stage is a geometrical definition of flat strips that will be assembled so as to realise the curved surfaces previously defined by the form-finding process.

Standard engineering analysis is then undertaken with a specific criterion; compression is not possible since it creates wrinkles. It should also be noted that the resultant effect of climatic actions and pre-stress is not an addition of their separate incidences but a combination, whose level is generally lower than their strict addition.

The membrane fabrication is also of great importance; how to design and size the plane strips so as to realise the designed shape when they are welded together and erected on site, is a major issue to solve.

EQUILIBRIUM OF CABLES AND MEMBRANES UNDER LOAD

Since it is possible to model a membrane using a cable net, it is useful to study the behaviour of a cable, which can only resist tension (the case of a rope in a tug of war). Without tension the cable is in a slackened state, losing its straight shape, which would give rise to wrinkles in the modelled membrane.

Theoretically speaking, straight horizontal cables cannot resist a vertical force (F) while beams can do so by flexion (2.5).

However it is possible to resist a vertical force with cables using a so-called "V shape". This V shape for cables is equivalent to the curvature of membranes. Curvature is dependant on the value of the initial angle α. If α increases, the tension decreases (T2 < T1) and since the associated cable deformation decreases, the stiffness increases (2.6). By analogy a flat, or nearly flat, membrane has zero or very low stiffness. Curvature is therefore necessary for stiffness, and in consequence local codes impose minimum values.

CURVATURE

The definition of a single curvature for a plane curve Cp is based on the properties of the circle defined by three points M, M' and M" on this curve. Geometrically speaking it can be established that when M' and M" get closer to M there is a unique circle of radius R that shares the same tangent line with the curve (2.7).

R is the radius of curvature of the curve at point M and $\rho = 1/R$ is the curvature. If R increases, ρ decreases (e.g. a flat curve has a zero curvature, R is infinite). The curvature is defined for each point of Cp.

2.7 ───

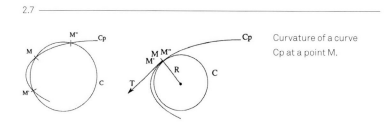

Curvature of a curve Cp at a point M.

For a spatial case like membrane surfaces, it is usual to define their "double curvature" at every point.

2.8 ───

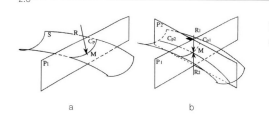

a   b

Double curvature of a surface at any point M.

If we consider a curved surface S intersected by a plane P_1, it is possible to define the curvature of the resulting curve Cp (radius R being defined as previously at point M for a single plane curve) (2.8 a).

According to the theory of geometry, there exist only two orthogonal planes P_1 and P_2 for which R_1 (in P_1) is maximal and R_2 (in P_2) is minimal (2.8 b). Planes P_1 and P_2 define the directions of the main curvatures; R_1 and R_2 are the corresponding main radii of curvatures. The parameter $K = 1/R_1 \cdot 1/R_2 (= \rho_1 \cdot \rho_2)$ is the total curvature at point M. If the centres of circles of radii R_1 and R_2 are not on the same side of the surface, it is an anticlastic shape (double negative curvature with $K < 0$). If the centres of circles are on the same side of the surface, it is a synclastic shape (double positive curvature, $K > 0$).

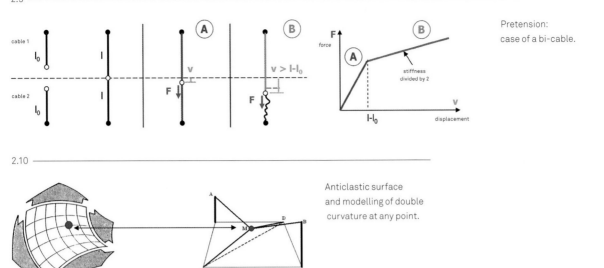

Pretension:
case of a bi-cable.

Anticlastic surface
and modelling of double
curvature at any point.

PRETENSION

Let us consider two cables of initial length equal to l_0. One of their ends is pinned and they are joined at their other end, having now a length l. Since l is greater than l_0, it is necessary during assembly to introduce a deformation in the cables by lengthening them, consequently introducing a pretension in the cables. When a force F is applied at the junction node, both cables initially contribute to the equilibrium, until a critical value of displacement v equal to $l-l_0$ (situation A in 2.9) is reached. After this specific value the lower cable slackens and no longer contributes to the equilibrium (situation B in 2.9). The stiffness (force divided by the displacement, i.e. the slope of the line) in situation B is half that of A.

COMBINATION OF PRETENSION AND CURVATURE

For every point on an anticlastic membrane, it is possible to model the double curvature with two inverted V shapes (AMB and CMD in 2.10) under pretension with the stiffness ensured in every direction.

A coupled action of curvature and pretension is then possible in order for efficient behaviour when combined with the effects of climatic actions. Local codes can impose a minimum value for the level of pretension. However, since it will be the only permanent action in the membrane, a maximum value should be considered in accordance with the fabric's tensile and fatigue strength. In practice, tension ranges from 100 to 300 daN/m.

It is beyond the scope of this chapter to give more information on the relationship between pretension values and radii of curvature, but interested readers can refer to scientific literature (see bibliography on page 228).

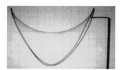

Form finding with soap films (ILEK Stuttgart, Germany).

FORM-FINDING

How to determine the surface shape of a membrane fixed at prescribed points and/or lines remained a difficult question for many years.[1] It is simultaneously necessary to introduce a pre-stress, whose level must be managed so as to avoid wrinkling or excessive tensions, while providing sufficient stiffness against climatic actions. The designer wishes also to dissipate water and has to verify the effective slope everywhere, keeping in mind the desired aesthetic.

The first step is to specify the anchoring points and lines: the top of a mast, fixed points (on the ground, on a wall...), straight lines, circular lines (top ring) and the perimeter for pneumatic membranes. Once these boundary conditions are defined, the form-finding process is performed with two main objectives: the surface definition and the pretension distribution, while not forgetting the design constraints.

Designers began to use known morphogenesis methods based on classical geometry and physical models ("historical models"). Nowadays, even if physical models are acceptable for preliminary studies, "numerical methods" are currently used.

ANALOGUE METHODS

Since the main constraint is to have a double-curved anticlastic surface for classic membranes (synclastic for pneumatic ones), designers can use geometrical strategies:

- combination of known surfaces;
- displacement of curves (one called the "director line", the other the "generator line");
- analytical methods (e.g. equation of the sphere or use of "splines" – curves that were used for naval architecture or the car industry).

Pioneers like Frei Otto worked with physical models, mainly with soap surfaces existing in a boundary frame[2] (2.11). These films under surface tension are of great interest since they are of minimum area and a quasi-homogenous state of pre-stress, consequently meeting the design constraints. It must however be underlined that the geometrical reproduction of the soap films was difficult (photogrammetry was used for some models) and that the associated morphological register was restricted, leading designers to look for other approaches.

 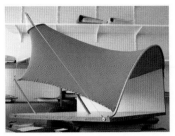 

Physical models
with Lycra.

Another method used is to create physical models using textiles (2.12). Even if they are quite impossible to transfer into a precise geometrical definition, they offer advantages like direct visualisation and the possibility of directly patterning on the model. They are still commonly used in the very early stages of design.

NUMERICAL METHODS

Several numerical methods were then developed to overcome the drawbacks of physical models. K. Linkwitz, who was involved in the Munich Olympic stadium project with Frei Otto (1972, 2.13) proposed the "Force Density Method" (FDM) that he developed with H.-J. Schek.[3] He modelled the membrane with a tensile cable net and designed it using FDM, which makes it possible to solve equilibrium equations using a prescribed linearisation: the engineer chooses the "force density coefficients" (tension/length ratio for each cable element connected to a net node).

For identical boundary conditions, different choices of these coefficients result in various shapes. This user-friendly method was quickly imported for tensile membrane form-finding, even though there are some key differences: distinction between the geometry of a tensile cable net and a tensile membrane, sensitivity to anchoring conditions, tension calculation in cable elements but not in a membrane. Further improvements followed such as the "surface density method".

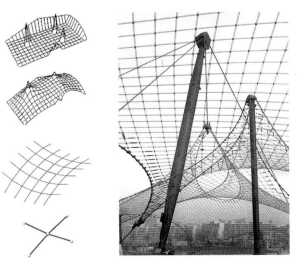

Force density method for cable nets form-finding. Left, form-finding process; right, realisation.

Another popular method, introduced by M. Barnes, is that of "Dynamic Relaxation" (DR)[4] in which equilibrium equations are solved by calculating a damped geometry in a dynamic process considering so-called "kinetic damping". A key feature of this method is that it is based on a surface modelling of the membrane and it gives the designer control of the pre-stress, for example to specify a uniform tension state (soap film).

A more classical method, the "Finite Element Method" (FEM), can also be used for surface modelling.[5,6] Two strategies are available:

- an initial shape "close to" the target one is prescribed and progressively modified by displacement of anchoring conditions. It is however difficult to evaluate the obtained form and tensions (the resulting shape is not always satisfactory: for instance, the existence of compressive areas) and this may require large calculation times;
- an initial shape is prescribed with a specification of the tension distribution. Here also, it is difficult to evaluate the obtained form and it is necessary to assess whether the tensions are compatible with an equilibrated shape.

Another efficient approach, also based on a surface modelling of the membrane, called the "Update Reference Strategy", has been developed more recently by K.-U. Bletzinger.[7]

PATTERNING

Like clothes that are the result of the assembly of cut flat pieces of fabric, the realisation of the membrane resulting from the form-finding process requires the definition of flat cut pieces. This definition is complex since many parameters must be taken into account. The first one is relative to the spatiality of the form: cutting lines are prescribed on a tridimensional shape to generate intermediate "strips". These strips are however not planar, and must be "flattened", since the fabricator has to cut them out of manufactured fabric rolls. Moreover, to satisfy the required pre-stress, they must be reduced before the final assembly by thermo-welding. This size reduction requires a very good knowledge of the geometric parameters and the mechanical characteristics of the fabric, itself an orthotropic material. An incorrect pattern definition may lead to wrinkles and areas of insufficient pre-stress. Even if several software applications are helpful in this operation, the designer's skill and experience remains the main guarantee of its success. Three operations are included in the patterning process: choice of the seam lines, flattening of a curved strip, and tension compensation by size reduction.

SEAMS

In order to manipulate seams and cutting lines the designer has to consider many parameters that can be classified as follows:

- technology: size of textile rolls (1.8 m wide for example), manufacturer's equipment (welding devices);
- cost: a higher number of seams will result in better accuracy but also in greater fabric cutting wastage;
- geometry: the total curvature represents the difficulty of mapping the surface onto a plane. A zone with high curvature may lead to smaller panels;

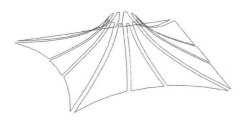

a Radial strips.
b Membrane for a dolphinarium (Parc Astérix, Paris, France).

a

b

– mechanics: a good knowledge of the main stress directions under loading is necessary to guide the positioning of the warp and weft directions (higher strength and rigidity in warp). Particular zones, mainly at boundaries may also govern the choice (connection to membrane edge cables or rigid rings, etc.). A common configuration uses radial strips (2.14 a);
– fabric behaviour: it is characterised by its orthotropic composition;
– aesthetics: a consistent visual rhythm is generally central for the architect (2.14 b).

The final choice is the result of compromises between all these parameters. Practically speaking, two main strategies are used to determine the seam lines:

– the use of geodesic lines (shortest path between two points, the equivalent of a "straight line" on a curved surface);
– the use of intersecting planes (e.g. vertical cut of surfaces).

The designer also has to be careful when larger sections are assembled as the number and size of strips on the connecting lines have to be equal.

FLATTENING

The objective is to determine the planar unfolded form of the strip (2D strip development) corresponding to the tridimensional strip defined on the surface after form-finding.
The variation of the total curvature K, previously defined as a geometric characteristic of surfaces, implies that there is no theoretical exact solution for double-curved membranes. The difference of K values shows the difficulty of transforming a curved surface into a planar one and vice-versa. With a flat sheet of paper it is possible to generate a cone or any other developable surface but it is impossible to create a sphere. The solutions proposed to map the Earth demonstrate this impossibility. Since there is no exact solution, different maps exist:

– equivalent flattening (preserves areas);
– equidistant flattening (preserves distances);
– conformal flattening (preserves angles: as with Mercator's map).

Nevertheless, it is impossible to simultaneously preserve the areas and lengths of a non-developable surface. The designer is therefore faced with the difficulty of transforming curved strips into planar surfaces in an operation known as "flattening". Several approaches based

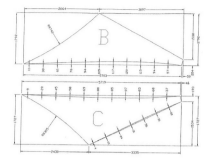

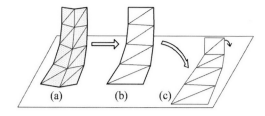

Flattening by simple triangulation.

on various optimisation techniques can be used (different approaches to minimise errors). It can be said that flattening causes more errors than form-finding. The simplest way is to use a simple triangulation (2.15).

COMPENSATION

If the strip sizes were strictly equal to the dimensions measured on the surface, the assembly of strips would not be in pretension after installation on site. It is consequently necessary to reduce the size of the strip in a "compensation" stage, which requires taking into account many factors:

- knowledge of the tension distribution (values defined in the form-finding) and textile behaviour (mechanical parameters in warp and fill directions: use of bi-axial tests);
- warp and weft compensation (0.2 to 5%) may be not identical and the orientation of the fabric relative to the seams is important;
- possible local compensation and de-compensation (depends on the context).
- long term behaviour and associated deformation: variation of tension in-situ (re-tensioning is generally necessary after several months).

From this it is clear that the patterning stage is critical for the design. It may produce errors in terms of seam determination, strip flattening and compensation, possibly resulting in difficulties in the erection and appearance of un-aesthetic wrinkles, but can also induce bad mechanical behaviour due to an inappropriate state of pretension.

 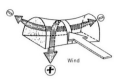 

Schematic equilibrium
of climatic actions
according to the double
curvature.

LOAD ANALYSIS

As for any construction the engineer has to proceed to a mechanical analysis of the membranes under load. The main external loads are climatic ones (wind and snow) and they will be combined with the effect of the internal pre-stress. Several indications result from this analysis:

- membrane deformation: governs the maximum deflection (generally limited by local codes);
- maximum membrane stress: determines the minimum fabric strength (and consequently validates the textile "type");
- direction of membrane stresses: important cue for seam line positioning and contiguous strip welding;
- maximum internal forces in the edge cables: allows choice of the minimum cable diameters;
- forces exerted on supports: required to dimension and design the main structural components (compressed masts and stays, loaded beams, anchorages, etc.).

The interaction between double curvature and pretension is taken into account at the design stage. The two directions of curvature play a role in balancing either wind or snow loads. The deformation of the membrane under a specified load induces variations in the pretension (2.16):

- the tension increases in one direction and decreases in the other one;
- if the membrane remains tensioned along these two directions, they both contribute to the stiffness;
- problems occur when the lower tension reaches a zero value: wrinkles appear and lead to membrane instability.

Normally, the pre-stress level ensures the absence of wrinkling. It could however occur for the case of high climatic actions (storm).

A textile membrane's stiffness is, of course, inferior to those of steel or concrete components. It is also dependent on the pre-stress level. Moreover, since displacements can be of high value, it is necessary to proceed to a "geometrical" non-linear analysis. The non-linear behaviour of the textile also necessitates adapting the stiffness to the deformation ("material" non linear analysis).

Consequently a non-linear analysis is always required, using a numerical iterative process (load is applied "step by step" in an incremental fashion).

CALCULATION UNDER SNOW

Snow is considered as a vertical load, uniformly distributed on the surface if there is no interaction with wind (no movement of snow over the membrane). The minimum values to be considered are prescribed by local codes.

It is not especially difficult to numerically calculate the behaviour under snow provided that there is no membrane wrinkling to generate instabilities.

2.17

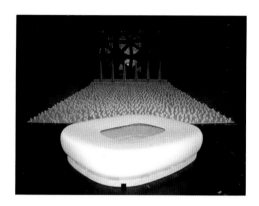 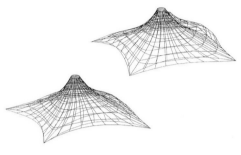

Study of wind effect (wind tunnel and cable net model).

CALCULATION UNDER WIND

The effect of wind, considered as a fluid, is always perpendicular to the surface, but the interaction between the wind and the shape of the structure generates zones under pressure and zones under suction. As for a conventional building, it is necessary to have a cartography of the external pressure coefficients C_e for the outside faces of the building; that will be combined with the effect of the wind inside the building (e.g. wind uplift) characterised by internal pressure coefficients C_i.

It is however generally difficult to evaluate the interaction between the membrane and the wind. Various approaches are available to evaluate the coefficients C_e and C_i:

- wind tunnel testing on models (2.17) (a good but laborious solution; scale effects can be sources of errors);
- empirical estimation of the resulting membrane coefficient C_e-C_i (depending on the engineer's experience);
- constant C_e-C_i values on the membrane (only acceptable if it results in a secure situation: the most unfavourable situation);
- computer calculation of C_e-C_i using dedicated software (this, however, necessitates careful assessment of the result).

ADDITIONAL LOADINGS

Other load cases are sometimes studied, such as dynamic earthquake analysis or natural wind vibrations. Specific assumptions are also necessary for the design of inflatable membranes (constant pressure or constant volume, etc.). The erection procedure may also require a specific study if it generates dangerous mechanical situations; this is mainly dependent on the local context.

CONCLUSION

Textile membrane design requires specific expertise from the designers at all stages: first sketches, form-finding, patterning and load analysis require close collaboration between architects and engineers. This partnership generally provides satisfying results in terms of architecture and cost.

1   Motro, R.; Maurin, B., "Membranes textiles architecturales. Comportement mécanique des systèmes tissés", in: Trompette, Ph. (ed.), Comportement mécanique des tissés, Cachan and London, Hermès-Lavoisier, 2006, p. 17-70.

2   Otto, F., Tensile Structures, vols. 1 and 2, Cambridge, MA, MIT Press, 1973.

3   Linkwitz, K.; Schek, H.J., "Einige Bemerkungen zur Berechnung von vorgespannten Seilnetzkonstruktionen", Ingenieur-Archiv 40, 1971, p. 145-158.

4   Barnes, M.R., "Applications of Dynamic Relaxation to the Design and Analysis of Cable, Membrane and Pneumatic Structures", in: 2nd International Conference on Space Structures, New York, Guildford, 1975.

5   Haug, E.; Powell, G.H., "Finite Element Analysis of Nonlinear Membrane Structures", in: IASS Pacific Symp. on Tension Structures and Space Frames, Tokyo and Kyoto, 1972, p. 124-135.

6   Haber, R.B.; Abel, J.F., "Initial Equilibrium Solution Methods for Cable Reinforced Membranes – Part I and II", Computer Methods. Applied Mech. Eng., vol. 30, 1982, p. 263-89 and p. 285-306.

7   Bletzinger, K.U.; Ramm, E., "A General Finite Element Approach to the Form Finding of Tensile Structures by the Updated Reference Strategy", International Journal of Space Structures, vol. 14, 1999, p. 131-246.

by BERNARD DORIEZ
and RENÉ MOTRO

③

DESIGN DETAILS FOR SUCCESSFUL IMPLEMENTATION

INTRODUCTION

Compared to traditional coverings, a tensioned technical textile structure transfers forces more directly to its fixings, concentrating the total force generated by the structure to its points of attachment.

Due to the tensile strength of reinforced fabrics, a textile structure can cover large spans without additional supporting frames. The membrane structure will thus concentrate all forces arising from climatic conditions, its self-weight and tensioning, onto the points of attachment. This concentration of forces requires that the design engineer and the fabric manufacturer must have detailed knowledge of the performance of the components used to make the anchorages.

The behaviour of the anchorages and the mechanisms that hold them in place is a key issue, and certainly the most important consideration for any technical textile application. Full-scale trials and practical experience gained during the construction of new projects can truly broaden the skills of the builders and engineers involved. The fittings, i.e. the mechanical components of the anchorage points, together with a suitable membrane tensioning system, must be designed to a size and specification that delivers the required strength and the necessary tension adjustments.

The examples presented, non-exhaustive by definition, show some possibilities of anchoring a membrane to its supporting structure. One should note that the range of possibilities is extensive, rendering standard solutions somewhat impractical. Each project, each membrane with its particular form, its integration into the actual site and the nature of the structure which will receive it, implies a new concept from the architect; and then from the engineer, who must adapt the detail and the dimensioning of the anchorage to the particular constraints.

IMPLEMENTATION CHALLENGES

Given the aforementioned conditions it is important to ensure precise design of the anchorages, which in turn provide a secure connection between the membrane and the rigid structural components. There are two requirements that designers need to focus on:

– ensuring conceptual and geometrical continuity between the membrane and the anchorage elements and,
– designing the anchorage elements to include, in most cases, mechanisms for tension adjustment.

The pretension comes from the characteristic shaping of an inverse double curvature and the modification of this form (in other words, stretching) by the anchorage elements. The adjustment mechanisms allow the level of tension to be attuned to the required level. It is this prestress that gives the membrane its rigidity.

Bad design and implementation of a textile membrane structure will result in a loss of rigidity, and in the occurrence of unattractive folds. These folds reveal the existence of compression zones in a membrane that should be in tension. They remain for the whole lifetime of the structure, whereas folds resulting from climatic conditions (wind and/or snow) are temporary. It is for this reason that a lot of care should be invested in the design, dimensioning and manufacture of the anchorages.

CLASSIFICATION OF TEXTILE MEMBRANES

The choice of a textile membrane's shape leads one to identify two classes according to their double curvature. Further choices concern the tensioning devices and especially the nature of the structures for which they are intended: peaks (mast heads or/and spars) and lines (rigid edges, flexible edges).

INFLATABLE SYSTEMS

Morphologically these correspond to systems with positive double curvature. After the first applications of the principle of inflatable envelopes by the Montgolfier brothers and Jean Baptiste Meusnier in 1783, there was no further important development until the 1940s. One can differentiate between airborne systems comprising a low-pressure double skin, and those that use tubes inflated to high pressure. The latter are not covered by this text; their anchorage methods are very specific.

SYSTEMS BASED ON EDGES AND PEAKS

Morphologically these correspond to systems with negative double curvature. The prestress of these systems can be achieved either:

- with linear style boundary conditions, rectilinear or curvilinear (made with rigid sides and/or flexible sides reinforced with "stiffening cables"). One thus obtains varied forms that allow the membrane to merge with other systems (for example, suspension from existing structures). The advantages of this type of solution include the possible division of the membrane, the attachment of partitioning elements, high durability for a low cost of ownership, ease of disassembly, as well as better sound insulation than that of inflatable systems. However, the necessary calculations are more difficult than for the class of systems based on positive double curvature. The pretension and its control require particular care. In certain cases it is necessary to provide lifting devices for adjacent constructions such as for example, three-dimensional arches;
- with point type boundary conditions through the use masts or spars, and related devices (load rings, rosettes, etc.). This type of solution allows larger spans and a larger range of shapes while retaining the ability of suspension from existing structures. The equilibrium surfaces are relatively complex and are subject to detailed calculations. The adjustment of pretension during the installation requires great care. In architectural terms, the closure solutions sometimes pose difficult problems. Careful control of pretension is therefore essential. From an architectural point of view it is sometimes very difficult to find solutions for membrane closure. As a consequence, careful checking of the prestress is essential.

TYPES OF APPLICATION

Tensioned technical textile membranes can be adapted to a wide variety of supporting structures. They can be specific to the application type, as in the case of the "Chinese hat" type project in 3.1. In this example the membrane is connected to a circular metal girder and to a central mast that generates the peak.

3.1

Membrane in the style of
a "Chinese hat".
Standalone solution.

System of metal and fabric: view from the outside and inner metal frame supporting the apex.

Membrane anchored onto existing buildings.

Architectural compositions also encourage the inclusion of combined metal - textile components combining metal frameworks and membranes. In the case shown (3.2) one or more height adjustable masts connect to a metal framework and form the peaks, while the membrane is laced over a tubular metal ring at its edge. The geometry of the contours is chosen by the designer; the choice determines the fabric panel cutting width.

One notes that in the first two projects presented, the design of the anchoring framework takes place in parallel with design of the membranes. This is not always the case; it is possible to anchor the membrane onto existing buildings (3.3). Of course, one must ensure that the forces thus generated can be balanced and dissipated by the existing structures .

CONNECTION DETAILS

The modeling and research of shape that the engineer undertakes using software designed to analyse the very specific behavior of tensile structures, defines the geometry of the membranes and their attachments to the anchorages. It is then necessary to develop the appropriate manufacturing detail for the membrane's attachment points.

In accordance with the technical and architectural specifications of each anchorage, the engineer develops the appropriate solution and designs the attachment detail. The manufacturer then applies his specialist knowledge of the fabric characteristics to realise membrane attachment points specific to the anchorage requirements.

LACING CORDS

This is a classical procedure (taken from sailing ship construction) for connecting the edges of a fabric membrane to a straight or slightly curved element. Holes are made in the fabric and reinforced by eyelets or metal plates; the cord goes through the eyelets and is laced to an element that is generally also made of metal (e.g. a plain circular rod), connected to the frame (3.21).

MEMBRANE CORNERS

Not all the edges of the textile membrane are straight, and in many cases stiffening cables are inserted into guides fixed along the textile borders. At a membrane corner, the tail ends of the two adjoining stiffening cables are connected to a carefully designed metallic plate, the "membrane corner plate". The corner plates must be precisely machined, as they frequently need to allow tensioning of the stiffening cables that support the membrane edges. The tension levels must be calculated such that the forces transmitted by the membrane corners are absorbed by the supports that receive them. All constituent parts must be correctly dimensioned: metal plate thickness, diameter of the threaded parts, bolts and shackles. The design of these fittings also contributes to the general appearance: if undersized it can result in a rupture (with catastrophic consequences), if oversized it detracts from the visual slenderness synonymous with technical textile-based structural systems.

DESIGN REQUIREMENTS FOR THE TECHNICAL DETAILS

The technical design of the membrane corner plates requires particular expertise. In the example show in figure 3.4, the coincidence of alignment of the two cables and the threaded central adjustment rod is ensured. In this case the forces in the two cables are not identical, resulting in a slight asymmetry concerning the plate angles, and also concerning the connection of the plate with the membrane, as indicated by the openings introduced for access to the tensioning bolts. One of the design difficulties lies in the requirement that the force lines should coincide. The engineer will be aware of this when designing the membrane corners, and must ensure this criterion in calculating the "in-service" tension conditions.

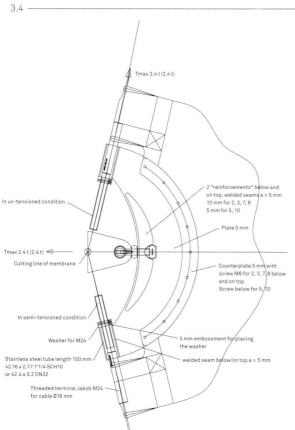

Tmax 3.4 t (2.4 t)

Membrane corner.
Technical details and
dimensions.

In un-tensioned condition

2 "reinforcements" below and
on top, welded seams a = 5 mm
10 mm for 2, 3, 7, 8
5 mm for 5, 10

Plate 5 mm

Tmax 3.4 t (2.4 t)

Cutting line of membrane

Counterplate 5 mm with
screw M6 for 2, 3, 7, 8 below
and on top
Screw below for 5, 10

In semi-tensioned condition

Washer for M24

5 mm embossment for placing
the washer

Stainless steel tube length 100 mm
42.16 x 2.77 1'1/4 SCH10
or 42.4 x 3.2 DN32

welded seam below/on top a = 5 mm

Threaded terminal Jakob M24
for cable Ø16 mm

Simple membrane corner.

SIMPLE CORNER

When the cable forces are weak it is possible to use a membrane corner without a complex tensioning mechanism (3.5). Assembly is simplified by directly attaching the two edge cables to the anchorage pole. Adjustment of the membrane tension is achieved by varying the tension of the guy "cables" securing the anchorage pole to the ground.

It is also possible to fix the membrane corner directly to the mast using an anchorage that comprises a shackle, a plate and a counter-plate (3.6). Fixing is made to a ring welded to the mast. It is nonetheless necessary to remember that such a connection at the central part of the mast induces internal bending forces where the mast is already anchored at the top. This solution is not suitable when large tension forces are required; not least because it is difficult to control the membrane tension, itself a function of the mast position.

ADJUSTABLE CORNER

A suitable adjustable solution would be a final design such as that seen in 3.7. In this example the two edge cables are provided with threaded end-pieces that pass through two twin tubes at the edges of the membrane corner plate before being secured by bolts. The metal plate itself is connected to the anchorage (pole or other) by a bolted threaded rod that passes through a third central tube integral with the plate.

3.6 ————————————————————————————————

Connection at a central part of the mast.

3.7 ————————————————————————————————

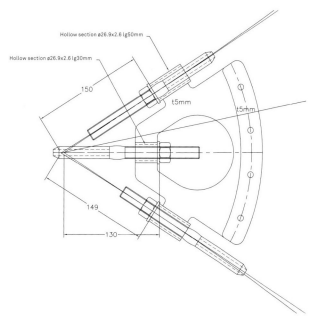

Membrane corner plate – fabrication detail.

Hollow section ø26.9x2.6 lg50mm

Hollow section ø26.9x2.6 lg30mm

150

t5mm

t5mm

t5mm

149

130

In figure 3.8 one can see the realisation of such a membrane corner. Also visible is a runoff pipe for rainwater. This is shown as an example of careless detailing. The rainwater will run directly over the metal plate and more particularly, over the screw threads giving rise to durability concerns, notwithstanding the use of corrosion resistant stainless steel. A simple solution is to extend the tube such that it passes through the metal plate to where the run-off water can be directed so as not to cause deterioration.

3.8

Membrane corner plate – installed.

MEMBRANE CORNER – MAST FIXING

In this design (3.9) the edge cables are of a fixed length without a system of adjustment. They are directly connected to the suspension plate that is fixed to the mast by shackles. Two chain plates (metal straps) provide the connection of the counter-plate to the plate. The arch-shaped counter-plate is bolted to the end of the membrane fabric. Tensioning the membrane is achieved by pulling the two guy cables that are fixed by metal lugs to the top of the mast.

3.9

Membrane corner – mast fixing.

NON-ADJUSTABLE EDGE CABLES

A second more rugged system with non-adjustable cables is illustrated in figure 3.10: two non-adjustable cables are connected to the traction plate, and a fabric strap sewn around a "delta" ring ensures that the membrane remains tight in the traction axis. In this system, as in the previous illustration, the membrane is also tensioned by one or several guy cables fixed to the mast.

3.10 ————————————————————————

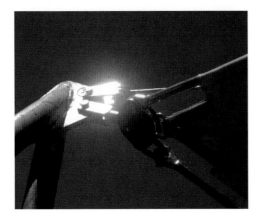

Non-adjustable edge cables.

3.11 ————————————————————————

Connection by shackle at the top of the mast.

SIMPLE MAST CONNECTION

A classic system of connecting a membrane corner to the top of a mast (3.11) consists of two edge cables that can be adjusted with threaded end-pieces, and a plate that is fixed to the mast by a shackle (here with a swivel to allow some rotation). Once again, the principal tension is regulated by adjusting the mast's guy cable; the tension of the membrane fabric is adjusted by the edge cables (by tightening the bolts holding the threaded cable ends). The membrane fabric has been reinforced by applying a double layer at its outer edges.

THE POLES

In the case of membranes secured by peripheral connection points, poles represent a classical choice for the lower connections (3.12).

3.12 ————————————————————————

The Dolphinarium covering at Parc Astérix, Paris, France.

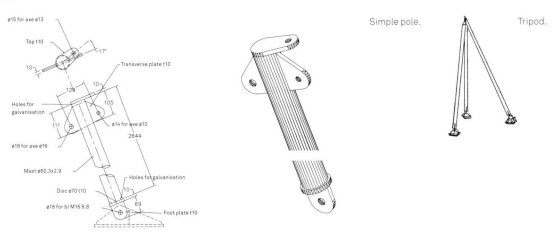

Simple pole.

Tripod.

The poles can be simple metal tubes (3.13). They are equipped with welded components that allow, at one end, a pin-joint connection, and at the other, lugs for connection of the membrane corner plates. The foot plate forms one of the two elements of the joint.

The poles are stabilised with two ropes that also serve to tension the structure. In some cases more complex solutions are used; combining three tubes together to form a tripod (3.14).

CENTRAL SUPPORTING MASTS

Elevated membrane supports can be achieved by the use of metal fixings and rosettes (rings) suspended from a mast, as is the case of the Dolphinarium at Parc Astérix (3.12). The mast must then be stabilised by guy cables. Central supporting masts are a solution for the creation of internal peaks. Generally used for structures in the style of "Chinese hats"; they are semi-hinged at the base with a threaded assembly allowing length adjustment (3.15). At the mast head, the membrane is secured by bolting the fabric between a circular plate and ring assembly (3.16).

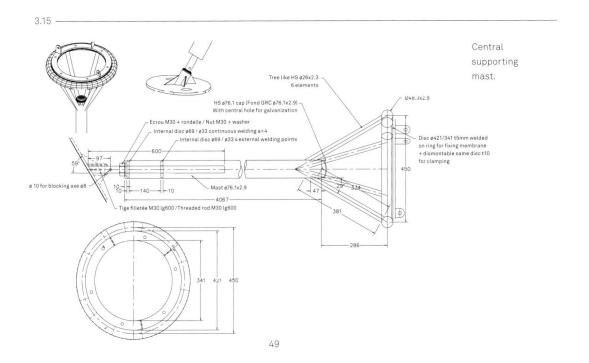

Central
supporting
mast.

Supporting device for
the peak.

The membrane is tensioned by adjustment of the mast height using the screw mechanism
at its base; to avoid overstressing the membrane it may be necessary, at the same time,
to adjust the stiffening cable tensions at the lower corner connections.

VARIANTS AND SPECIFIC TECHNICAL SOLUTIONS

By adapting technical solutions to current projects, the designer can produce a multiplicity
of options. He must keep in mind the general requirements concerning mechanical connections, while proposing shapes and dimensions that are in harmony with the general
architectural principles of membrane structures. A principal requirement of this type
of structural system is achieving the required membrane tension, indispensable for its
rigidity. This is a field where the creativity of the designer is at the forefront: the proposed
solutions will determine not only the ease of construction, but also the resulting costs.
While not exhaustive, selected examples are given in the following section.

STRUCTURAL CHOICES: FORM AND CONNECTION

FAÇADE CANOPIES

Canopy on curved arches
The first example shows a sun-protection canopy over a glass façade. The covering fabric
is associated with a series of gently curved arches. It is bordered at the front edge by
curved cables and laced at the rear to the straight coping while following the profile of the
façade. The arches are grouped in pairs and connected by a horizontal tube, thus forming
a cross-linked system containing two pairs of connected V-shaped crossbars. They are
joined to the top façade panel and also to the tops of beams that are integrated in the
façade. Cables in the form of Saint Andrew's crosses ensure bracing (3.17).

Canopy on curved arches.

"Flying" struts

The impression of lightness can be underlined by the use of metal tubes of which at least one end is stabilised by a grouping of a minimum of three cables. These completely compressed tubes are called struts. This solution was adopted for the canopy topping the façade in 3.18. The tensioning here is ensured by the struts, with toggles and turnbuckles allowing a connection at the outer corners of the canvas. The struts are tied to the façade by guy wires.

3.18

"Flying" struts.

3.19

"Flying masts".

If the two ends of the compressed tube are connected to the suspension system, this gains even greater freedom in space, and can even be regarded as a "flying mast". In the case shown in figure 3.19 the upper tensioning system is simply the membrane itself. It is necessary to provide a metal collar reinforcement in order to distribute the force and to avoid penetrating the fabric.

GRANDSTANDS AND SHELTERS

Having a completely unrestricted view or unilateral access to a building in one unbroken line are imperatives of classical architecture. In this context Eduardo Torroja contributed a masterful solution with his concrete shells for the La Zarzuela horse racecourse in Madrid. Textile membranes offer structural and morphological solutions that mirror Torroja's example. In these two structures, the grandstand of a stadium (3.20) and a bicycle shelter (3.21), the scales may be different, but in both cases you can find an inclined supporting frame supplied with two parts that serve as suspension lines holding the tubes to which the membrane is laced. The stability of the construction requires the installation of tie bars at the rear to counteract the cantilever forces.

3.20 —————————————————————————

Stadium grandstand: "horse saddle" membrane laced at the edge.

3.21 —————————————————————————

Bicycle shelter.

INNOVATIVE DETAILS

The relevance of the choice of solutions connecting the membrane to the support often depends upon the coherence of the design: it is necessary to combine the separate connection elements to a homogenous unit in terms of dimensioning as well as from an aesthetic point of view (3.22).

3.22

Design for the connection of fabric, corner plate and concrete pole.

The open design of the fabric corner plate offers a lighter visual impression that offsets the imposing dimensions of the concrete support.

It is always the task of the designer to propose innovative solutions; for example, creating a tensioning system that is in harmony with the project being undertaken. The following two suggestions were made and developed for tensioning a continuous edge cable (3.23 and 3.24).

An ingeniously simple tensioning system, placed at the ends of an arch, allows the use of one single length of stiffening cable extending from one end to the other, with intermediate tension adjusters.

3.23

3.24

Simple tensioning system for continuous stiffening cable.

Continuous edge stiffening cable retained at the end of the strut.

Creating tension by
weighting the membrane.

Construction "lightened"
by thin cables.

BUT ALSO ...

Particular project specifications can generate very special technical solutions. A unique system: ballast bags filled with sand create the required tension through their own weight applied to the gantries at the membrane's extremities. This solution was devised in response to the impossibility of ground anchorages at this archaeological site (3.25).

The delicacy of textile construction also places demands on the other elements. In order to avoid the use of massive arches to support the membrane, the designer established an intermediate supporting system similar to that historically developed by Polonceau, and whose name it bears. This design makes use of practically invisible cables attached to two slender "deltas" that together contribute to the structure's lightness (3.26).

And after that, it only remains to let the sails join the realm of the birds by reducing to an absolute minimum their connection to the supporting masts (3.27). Here the contrasting colours between the membranes and masts contribute greatly to this impression.

Sails suspended by
wind-braced masts.

CONCLUSION

It is clear that the use of technical textiles provides architectural solutions that offer significant savings in material resources. The design of the technical details for their implementation requires specific skills on the part of the engineer: imagination, a mechanical background and technological experience. The engineer's role is to ensure the transition from concept to final construction; economy of material set against expenditure of grey matter.

by STEFANO BERTINO,
ANDREA GIOVANNI MAININI
and TIZIANA POLI

TEXTILE FAÇADES

Innovation is a prerequisite for every project. Textile façades are born of such an objective; far from ephemeral they represent a means of realising durable and high performance architectural solutions. The main goals for the designer are assessing the different and complex "surface tensile stresses", checking sophisticated frame details and developing new structural concepts and shapes. Textile architecture and textile building envelopes are the result of continuous study aimed at balancing many different constraints.

TEXTILE ENVELOPE: PERFORMANCE AND APPLICATION FIELDS

Independent of the chosen technical solutions and the structural design criteria, the additional architectural considerations are:

- optimal comfort conditions for end-users of the indoor living space (hygrothermal, acoustic and visual comfort, air quality);
- the resistance to static loads self-weight, snow and dynamic loads (wind, earthquake and shock);
- fire resistance;
- impermeability under the combined action of rainwater and wind;
- the control of vapour diffusion and condensation phenomena;
- the required thermal insulation;
- control of light transmission to indoor spaces;
- control of solar radiation (control of solar heat gain);
- sound reduction index;
- the integration and installation of service plant;
- the required service life;
- reduction of the environmental impact.

While the above considerations are all resolved by a textile envelope structure it is necessary to consider a range of additional performance issues related to: the maintainability (surface cleaning), the substitutability, the surface interface forces between different textile components and its behaviour under load transfer to primary and secondary structural support elements.

CONI, Sport Center Building, Bergamo, Italy. Textile envelope as an architectural skin.

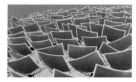

Artificial Ivy in Tefzel with PV cell (ETFE modified by DuPont).

Enlargement of the Santa Giulia Museum, Brescia, Italy. Example of a full textile envelope. The approach of mimesis deceives the observer until he or she comes into contact with the surface.

New Tensoforma Trading Srl office building, Entratico, Italy. Textile components as a solar shading device.

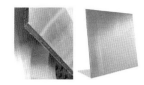

Energain DuPont.

Furthermore it is important to control:

- component deformations under dynamic wind action;
- maximum thermal expansion for each component;
- strain of every structural component (including primary and secondary components) under applied loads;
- load concentrations on lower mechnically resistant facade areas;
- moisture absorption and thermal stress endurance;
- mechanical and geometrical compatibility of the elements in every assembly or interface;
- dimensional tolerances.

The level of control undertaken depends upon the type of application. Textile building envelopes can be realised as static systems (finishes), as adaptable systems (full textile envelopes) or to enhance façade performance (adaptive active second skin) according to the environment. We can thus differentiate between the following applications:

- air and water permeable layer (skin) applied in adhesion to the structure's outer insulating layer working as an external surface finishing system (textile-coated façade);
- textile layer applied as an external surface finish using a mechanical fastening system. The inter-layer cavity ventilation level can vary from none to high (4.1);
- textile layer variously permeable to light and air with a solar protection function (solar transmission control, luminous flux control, thermal resistance increase) (4.2);
- textile layer that can transform or produce energy (amorphous photovoltaic [PV] integration) (4.3);
- a building envelope system, resilient, adaptive and multilayer (full textile envelope) (4.4, 4.5).

A more precise classification is given in terms of the specific performance enhancement for each type of application.

Categories		Figure (see p. 59)	Control of thermal transmittance	Control of total solar transmission	Control of light transmittance	Added thermal resistance	Control of vapour condensation on surfaces	Soundproofing behaviour	Noise absorption	Energy recovery, production and transformation	Architectural solution
Second textile layer	Textile layer (skin) adhesion with outer insulating layer	1					• Breathable, waterproof membrane				•
	Second textile layer mechanically fixed to inner wall surface	2		•		•	• Breathable, waterproof membrane		•	• Coupling with PV cells	•
	Second textile layer as solar protection	3		•	•	•				• Coupling with PV cells	•
	Second textile layer coupled with OLED (Organic Light-Emitting Diode)	4			•						•
Textile envelope/façade	Two coupled textile layers enclosing an air gap or cavity	5	•	•	•			•	•		•
	Two coupled textile layers covering an insulating layer	6						•	•		•
	Two coupled textile layers enclosing a cavity. One or two internal surfaces of the cavity have a low-emissivity coating	7	•	•	•						•
	Three textile layers, enclosing two cavities filled with insulating material	8						•	•		•
	Two coupled textile layers enclosing a cavity. The external surface is covered with PV cells	9	•	•	•					•	•
	Three textile layers, enclosing two cavities filled with insulating material. External surface covered with PV cells	10						•	•	•	•
	Three textile layers, creating two cavities filled with air or high insulating gas	11	•	•	•						•
	Three textile layers, creating two cavities filled with air or high insulating gas. Internal cavities surfaces have a low-emissivity coating.	12	•	•	•						•
	A twin layer pneumatic cushion filled with air	13	•	•	•						•
	A two layer pneumatic cushion filled with an insulating material	14						•	•		•
	A three layer pneumatic cushion filled with air	15	•	•	•						•

Building textile envelope type and performance. (Source: T. Poli)

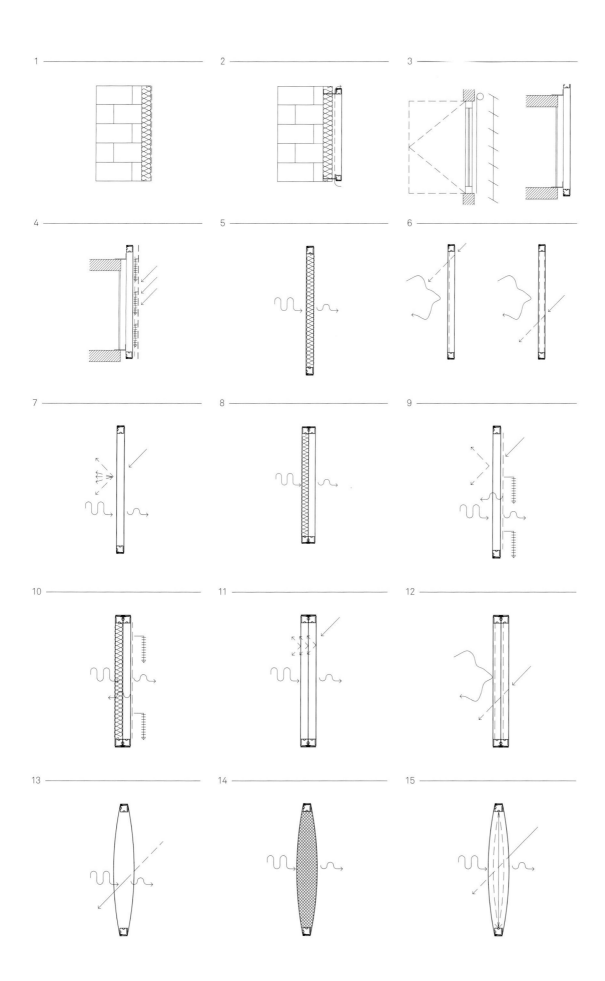

TEXTILE BUILDING ENVELOPE SYSTEMS FOR DIFFUSE ARCHITECTURE

Textile envelope solutions can have great scenic and architectural impact, such as the UBPA B3-2 Pavilion at the EXPO 2010 in Shanghai or the Juventus FC Arena in Turin, where "ad hoc" architectural designs have been adopted. The range of textile envelope applications is enhanced by greater flexibility when compared to glass façade technology. Glass, a rigid and fragile material, is replaced with a flexible and high strength textile element; verification of structural internal forces now involves different variables, particularly in relation to the behaviour of the textile envelope.

For example, Tensoforma has developed and patented TEXO, a structural system based on the use of an elastomeric edge detail interposed between the textile and the chassis, usually constituted by a hot extruded aluminium profile equipped with a thermal break and a system of seals and gaskets that provide waterproofing and the control of air flow. The elastomeric edge detail (4.6, 4.7) produces a uniform and smooth textile surface while its elasto-plastic behaviour allows the redistribution of applied loads. The textile membrane is connected by sewing to the elastomeric edge detail, which is then inserted into an appropriate slot in the aluminium profile. The elastomer acts as a "spring", providing uniform modular elements and the redistribution of applied loads, while allowing the possibility of future changes to the textile envelope.

4.6, 4.7 ───

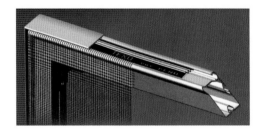 

"Diffuse" technology of textile building components.

The modularity of this type of building envelope is not synonymous with standard forms or sizes; many different forms and functions may be attained using the textile panels. The lack of constraint imposed by a textile building envelope system allows free reign to the designer's architectural sensitivity, providing a wide variety of individual technical solutions (4.8 – 4.13).

Private house, Vienna, Austria. The textile envelope has a double function: architectural skin and solar shading device.

Deichmann Store, Essen, Germany.

Centro Italmoda, Endine-Bergamo, Italy.

PRADA Store, Quingdao, China.

3M, Sensitive Space System, Salone internazionale del mobile, Milan, Italy. Texo system for interior.

Fabbrica – les yeux ouverts – Centre Pompidou, Paris, France. Texo system for interior.

4.12

4.13

UBPA B3-2 Pavilion at
EXPO 2010, Shanghai,
China. Archea Associati.

America's Cup Base
Lunarossa, Valencia,
Spain. Renzo Piano
Building Workshop.

TEXTILE BUILDING ENVELOPE LIMITATIONS

The low weight, good strength and high-performance versatility of textile envelopes does present some important issues in relation to the design, construction and maintenance phases. The design of textile envelopes requires a good knowledge of materials science and technology. Not all textiles behave in the same way (i.e. elongation resistance) and not all textiles retain their physical integrity and performances over a long period. Furthermore, the installation of textile envelopes cannot be done by unskilled workers. The low fire resistance of textile materials must also be balanced by a high fire resistance of load-bearing elements and elements that link the membrane to the main structure (i.e. polycarbonate). Textiles facades have additional safety problems due to a low resistance to local mechanical stresses if the fabric is not reinforced.

PERFORMANCE CHECKLIST FOR BUILDING DESIGNERS

The use of textiles as a whole building envelope system, or as an external second skin, is increasing. Due to the importance of the building envelope, being responsible for the most significant characteristics affecting the building's use, checklists of the required environmental and technical performance characteristics are given. The use of textiles as intermediate layers for lightweight walls is also an option; as such they are included in the range of possible applications.

ENVIRONMENTAL PERFORMANCE

A checklist for environmental performance and user comfort

| | | | INTERMEDIATE LAYER | | SECOND LAYER | | | | TEXTILE ENVELOPE | |
| | | | LIGHTWEIGHT WALL | | TRANSPARENT WALL | | OPAQUE WALL | | MULTILAYER TEXTILE WALL | |
REQUIRED PERFORMANCE			Frame	Textiles	Frame	Textiles	Frame	Textiles	Frame	Textiles
ENVIRONMETAL PERFORMANCE	COMFORT	Acoustic insulation[4]								•
		Light control				•				•
		Night time privacy				•				•
		Visual contact with the outside				•				•
		Glare control				•				•
		Rendering of colours				•				•
		Water tightness[1,3]	•	•	•	If requested	•	If requested	•	•
		Water impermeability[1,3]	•	•	•	If requested	•	If requested	•	•
		Natural ventilation capability[2]				•		•		•

Intermediate layer

1 Water tightness and water impermeability protects intermediate and internal layers of the wall from degradation by water. The intermediate layer can also be used as a vapour barrier to prevent vapour diffusion in a lightweight wall.

Second layer

2 Natural ventilation capability is recommended to avoid green house effects in the gap between the second textile skin and the wall (transparent and opaque). Natural ventilation of the gap also reduces solar gain and cooling loads.

3 Combined water tightness and water impermeability are generally not obtined by the external second skin alone but in conjunction with the traditional transparent or opaque wall behind.

Textile envelope

4 Acoustic insulation is critical for textile envelopes, especially for multilayer pneumatic structures. The absence of a massive layer, beyond a low sound reduction index, could give rise to low sound insulation and tiresome noise from the impact of raindrops.

TECHNICAL PERFORMANCE

A checklist for technical performance

| | | | INTERMEDIATE LAYER | | SECOND LAYER | | | | TEXTILE ENVELOPE | |
| | | | LIGHTWEIGHT WALL | | TRANSPARENT WALL | | OPAQUE WALL | | MULTILAYER TEXTILE WALL | |
REQUIRED PERFORMANCE			Frame	Textiles	Frame	Textiles	Frame	Textiles	Frame	Textiles
TECHNICAL PERFORMANCE	THERMAL	Solar factor				•				•
		Direct solar transmittance				•				•
		Secondary heat transfer factor				•		•		•
		Solar radiation reduction factor				•		•		•
		Solar gain control [3,4]				•		•		•
		Thermal loss reduction		If requested	•	•	•	•	•	•
		Air permeability [1,2]		If requested		If requested		If requested	•	•
		Air tightness [1,2]		If requested		If requested		If requested	•	•
		U-value [6,5]							•	•

Intermediate layer

1 In well-insulated buildings the major thermal loss in winter depends upon ventilation and air infiltration. A continuous airtight layer could reduce air infiltration from the outside.

Second layer

2 In well-insulated buildings (average wall and roof U-value < 0.3 W/m² K) the major amount of thermal loss in winter depends primarily on ventilation and air infiltration. A continuous external textile skin could reduce wind pressure on the transparent or opaque wall behind, reducing air infiltration from the outside.

3 Solar gain through the windows dominate cooling loads in air-conditioned buildings. The use of a textile second skin can reduce solar gains, reducing cooling loads and energy consumption. The amount of the reduction depends on the glazed portion of the façade and on the solar factor of the textile. A very low solar factor for textile surfaces adjacent to a transparent wall could reduce solar gain while also reducing light transmission, with resultant reduction in daylight autonomy and consequential increase in energy use for internal lighting.

Textile envelope

4 Translucent materials may be used to control solar gains. If 98% sunlight-transparent membranes are used, it is necessary to reduce solar gain using adaptive or passive shading systems. Diffuse serigraphy of one or more layers of the envelope is also a useful strategy for controlling solar gain.

5 Thermal transmittance U control is critical for multilayer textile envelopes. This kind of envelope has a thermal transmittance U between 3.3 W/m² K (2 layers) and 1.9 (5 layers). The thermal transmittance value can be reduced by using membranes or textiles with a low emissivity surface treatment. Metal frames should incorporate thermal breaks (insulation), to reduce conduction losses through the system.

6 The use of a textile layer with low emission surfaces in a cavity between two different wall surfaces, increases thermal resistance of the cavity and reduces thermal transmittance of the wall

| | | | INTERMEDIATE LAYER | | SECOND LAYER | | | | TEXTILE ENVELOPE | |
| | | | LIGHTWEIGHT WALL | | TRANSPARENT WALL | | OPAQUE WALL | | MULTILAYER TEXTILE WALL | |
REQUIRED PERFORMANCE			Frame	Textiles	Frame	Textiles	Frame	Textiles	Frame	Textiles
TECHNICAL PERFORMANCE	DURABILITY	Colour fastness			•	•	•	•	•	•
		No degradation of appearance			•	•	•	•	•	•
		Resistance to breakage			•	•	•	•	•	•
		Corrosion resistance					•		•	
		Ultraviolet light resistance				•		•		•
		Biological agent resistance	•	•	•	•	•	•	•	•
		Ageing resistance	•	•	•	•	•	•	•	•
		Fire resistance [1]							•	•
		Moisture resistance	•	•	•	•	•	•	•	•
		Water resistance	•	•	•	•	•	•	•	•

Textile envelope

1 Fire resistance is critical for multilayer textile envelopes. The materials are generally treated to prevent burning, with toxicity levels guaranteed for different degrees of fire exposure. The toxicity for the user depends on the amount of burning material because all plastics release dioxin and other toxic substances when they burn.

The resistance to fire is low, hence it is important to define adequate separations of enclosed volumes and structures to prevent rapid spread of fire through the building.

			INTERMEDIATE LAYER		SECOND LAYER				TEXTILE ENVELOPE	
			LIGHTWEIGHT WALL		TRANSPARENT WALL		OPAQUE WALL		MULTILAYER TEXTILE WALL	
REQUIRED PERFORMANCE			Frame	Textiles	Frame	Textiles	Frame	Textiles	Frame	Textiles
TECHNICAL PERFORMANCE	MECHANICAL	Impact resistance			•	•	•	•	•	•
		Wind resistance			•	•	•	•	•	•
		Tensile stress resistance			•	•	•	•	•	•
		Intruder resistance [2]							•	•
		Cutting resistance [1]				•		•		•

Second layer

1   Cutting resistance is critical for a textile second layer, and in particular against vandalism. To provide cutting resistance the textile may be coupled with plexiglass or other plastics. Textiles with added metal fibres may also be used.

Textile envelope

2   Intruder resistance is critical for textile second layers and in particular against vandalism.

TEXTILE ENVELOPE'S FUTURE FOR LOW ENVIRONMENTAL IMPACT BUILDINGS

The long-term environmental impact analysis of a product is complex and needs to acknowledge that the analysis of sustainable textile architecture, purely in terms of recyclability and a low emission of toxic substances is no longer adequate.

Nowadays sustainable materials have to respect the environment during their whole life cycle, for which the constraints are:

– use of natural resources – water use and consumption for production – energy consumption for production – energy consumption for transport and execution	Commonly defined as the standard of the material
– greenhouse gasses for climate warming emissions – toxicity for humans and the environment – common and hazardous waste	

The definition of all sustainability indicators is complex because of: lack of information, and the inter-disciplinary nature of the study necessary for a thorough analysis.

However, products are available that, while maintaining the characteristics of high durability and mechanical strength, are "purged" of toxic chemicals.

The major components of a textile building envelope system may be recycled, reducing the consumption of natural resources and energy:

New industrial processes for separating textile components from coatings makes it possible to recycle of a wide range of textiles (Texyloop system, developed by Ferrari S.A.). At the end of the service life the materials may be re-used in a virtuous cycle, re-using raw materials to make new products.

Notwithstanding the high energy, material and water consumption during production, steel and aluminium frames have a high recycling index enabling them to be molten and re-used.

The use of lightweight materials for textile envelopes also reduces the energy consumption for transportation; textiles can be easy rolled for packaging hence optimising the use of space on trains, planes and trucks.

The sustainability of a textile building envelope system when equipped with a second layer may also be enhanced, depending on the application, by a secondary effect. The building's envelope is responsible for the major cost of heating and cooling the interior, the main loads being:

- building envelope infiltration (winter);
- conduction losses (winter and summer) and;
- solar gain (summer).

Depending upon the building's shape factor, average wall insulation level, and the ratio between transparent and opaque wall areas, the application of a well-designed textile second layer can substantially decrease these annual costs.

by MARK COX, TIM DE HAAS,
ROEL GIJSBERS, ARNO PRONK,
IVO VROUWE and JEROEN
WEIJERS

SOLAR PROTECTION

INTRODUCTION

Textile applications can be used in different ways to establish climate control, for example:

- by the use of special materials (phase-changing materials) or coatings;
- by the use of multiple layers of textile;
- by heating or cooling of the membranes;
- by cooling through ventilation of air through the membrane.

A membrane can function in different ways. It can be used as a means of solar protection or for the purpose of thermal and acoustic insulation. Solar protection devices are used to prevent solar heating. Non-transparent membranes and multiple-layer membranes are suitable for this purpose. The thermal insulation value of the construction depends on the thickness of the membranes and of the spaces between the membranes. Better insulation can be achieved by using transparent material or reflecting layers.

Heat transfer has become a key issue in building design. In this contribution the basic heat transfer principles will be discussed and the relations between them explained. On the basis of these principles we will describe the different methods of climate control with regard to membrane constructions.

KEY TERMS ON SOLAR PROTECTION

Single-layer textile
Material woven or knitted into one single layer, with poor acoustic and thermal insulation properties.

Multi-layer textile
Material woven or knitted into double or multi-layers, with potential acoustic and thermal insulation properties.

Multi-layer insulated membrane roof
Cushions consisting of two or more layers of ETFE membranes with encapsulated air. The heated air contained between the layers provides thermal and acoustic insulation. The air inside the cushion is heated by solar energy. It can be extracted and used to heat the building.

Air-open membrane
A membrane through which air can move freely.

Air tightness
The resistance of the building envelope to inward or outward air leakage. Low air tightness will result in the increase of energy consumption to compensate for air leakage. Therefore, air tightness is a major factor in current building design.

Transparent membrane
A membrane through which visible light can pass.

Ventilation
The use of air as a transport medium for cooling or heating. The air can be preheated while contained between membranes.

Solar transmittance
The percentage of incoming solar radiation that passes through a transparent material. Single-pane glass has a solar transmittance of approximately 0.8, i.e. 80% of the solar radiation is transmitted through the glass.

Visible light transmittance
The percentage of incoming visible light that passes through a material, weighted by the sensitivity of the human eye. Single-pane glass has a visible light transmittance of approximately 0.9.

Black body
A theoretical radiation source that absorbs all radiation, thus reflecting and transmitting none.

BASIC HEAT TRANSFER PRINCIPLES

Heat transfer is an important factor when textiles are used for solar protection. There are three main heat transfer principles: radiation, convection and transmission.

RADIATION EMISSION AND RADIATORS

Any material with a specific temperature acts as a radiation source. The emitted radiation equals the absorbed radiation according to Kirchhoff's law (5.1).

5.1 ─────────────────────────

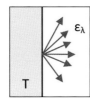

$\varepsilon_\lambda = \alpha_\lambda$

Emitted radiation (ε_λ)
by a material.

The emitted radiation differs according to wavelengths, thus forming a spectrum. This spectrum is related to the temperature of a black body, a theoretical radiation source, and is defined by radiation Planck's law.

$$I(v,T) = \frac{2hv^3}{c^2} \frac{1}{e^{hv/kT}-1}$$

I(v,T) = emission for frequency and temperature		[Wm^{-2}SrHz]
v = frequency		[Hz]
T = temperature		[K]
c = speed of light	2.99792458 · 10^8	[m/s]
k = Boltzmann constant	1.386505 · 10^{-23}	[J/K]
h = Planck constant	6.6260693 · 10^{-34}	[Js]

The spectrum of emitted radiation can be visualised in an intensity curve. The surface under an intensity curve equals the total emitted radiation of the material and will be larger at a higher temperature. The total emitted thermal radiation is defined by Stefan-Boltzmann's law:

$E_T = \varepsilon_\lambda \cdot \sigma \cdot T^4$		[W/m^2]
ε_λ	= emission coefficient for wavelength λ	[-]
σ	= Stefan-Boltzmann's constant = 5,669 · 10^{-8}	[W/m^{2}K^4]
T	= temperature	[K]

There are three principles to describe a radiation source: a black body, a grey body or a selective radiator (5.2).

- A black body has an emission coefficient of 1. It absorbs all radiation, thus reflecting and transmitting none.
- A grey body radiator has an emission coefficient which is lower than 1 and is constant for every wavelength.
- A selective radiator has different emission coefficients for every wavelength and is lower than 1.

5.2

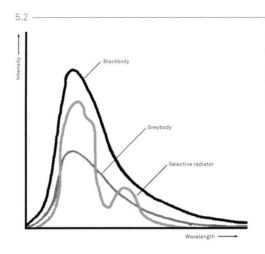

Radiation emission of different radiators; black body (black), grey body (grey) and selective radiator (green).

The spectrum of the sun is slightly different from the spectrum of a black body with a temperature of 5800 K. Also, the atmosphere of the earth filters out some light in various wavelengths, resulting in gaps in the spectrum. Stefan-Boltzmann's law, which defines the total emitted thermal radiation, refers to a perfect black body, so that the value acquired by employing this formula is higher than what will occur in reality (5.3).

5.3

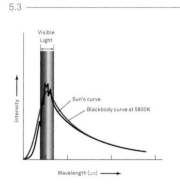

Intensity curves of emitted radiation of the sun and of a black body with a temperature of 5800 K.

5.4

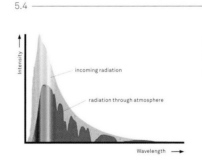

Intensity curve of radiation showing the filter effect of the atmosphere.

The mean total radiation, i.e. the total of direct and diffuse radiation at a vertical surface in the summer, taking the example of the Netherlands, is approximately 400 W/m^2 [Knoll, 2002].

Membranes in general and textiles in particular are not perfect black body emitters because they reflect light. As a result not all light is absorbed, and in the case of transparent materials, light can pass through them. Non-transparent membranes and textiles act more like grey body radiators, while transparent membranes act more like selective radiators. These properties can be used to block the infra-red radiation – heat – while allowing visible light to pass.

Non-transparent materials
A non-transparent material absorbs and reflects incoming radiation. The material acts as a grey radiator, in this example, with a temperature of 80°C on the inside of the building (5.5).

5.5

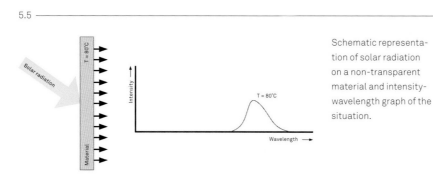

Schematic representation of solar radiation on a non-transparent material and intensity-wavelength graph of the situation.

Transparent materials
A transparent material allows solar radiation to pass though it causing heat generation, usually called passive solar energy. Here one can clearly discern the importance of solar protection (5.6).

5.6

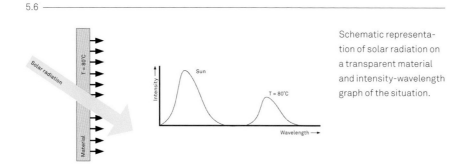

Schematic representation of solar radiation on a transparent material and intensity-wavelength graph of the situation.

Coatings are important in the radiation-heat transfer process because they can provide selective radiator properties. The amount of reflection and emission is influenced by surface properties like roughness and colour. Rough surfaces reflect less radiation than smooth surfaces and dark colours have a higher emission coefficient than light colours. Transparent membranes have a high transmitting coefficient because they allow light to pass through easily.

RADIATION

Radiation can be divided into the visible and the invisible spectrum. The visible spectrum comprises radiation with wavelengths ranging from 0.4 to 0.8 μm. Radiation occurs at smaller wavelengths, called ultraviolet light and larger wavelengths of 0.8 to 800 μm, defined as infrared light. Radiation heat transfer is mainly caused by infrared radiation because of the larger intensity of these wavelengths in the solar spectrum (5.3 and 5.4).

Three material properties are important factors with regard to the incoming radiation with wavelength λ: absorption α_λ, reflection ρ_λ, transmission τ_λ. The sum of these three components is always 1, representing the amount of incoming radiation (5.7). A non-transparent material does not transmit radiation.

5.7

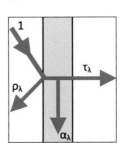

$\alpha_\lambda + \rho_\lambda + \tau_\lambda = 1$
Incoming radiation (1); absorption (α_λ), reflection (ρ_λ), transmission (τ_λ).

Example		Solar radiation on a single layer of transparent PVC membrane	
Incoming radiation		800 W/m²	
Absorption (α_λ)	20%	160 W/m²	leading to an increase of the temperature of the membrane
Reflection (ρ_λ)	10%	80 W/m²	
Transmission (τ_λ)	70%	560 W/m²	

CONVECTION

In the case of air flowing over a surface, heat is transferred by convection (5.8). An air flow can be produced by mechanical installations or originate from temperature conditions or pressure differences. The energy flow by convection depends on the heat transfer coefficient at the surface, which equals the size of the surface in contact with the air and the difference between surface temperature and air temperature. The heat transfer coefficient at the surface is related to the dynamic viscosity of the air, the air speed and the property of the airflow, either laminar or turbulent. Convection is used in façade construction with multiple layers of textiles for extracting the heat between the different layers.

$Q = \alpha \times A(T_s - T_a)$	[W]
Q = heat current by convection	[W]
α = convection coefficient	[W/m²K]
A = surface	[m²]
T_s = surface temperature	[K]
T_a = air temperature	[K]

5.8 ──────────────────────

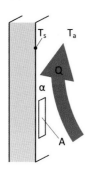

$Q = \alpha \cdot A(T_s - T_a)$
Heat transfer by convection.

Example   Convection along a surface in a single-membrane construction

$Q = \alpha \cdot A(T_s - T_a)$ [W]

Solar irradiation will make the membrane warm up, thus causing a higher surface temperature. When using multiple layers and an air cavity, the surface temperature and consequently the heat current by convection will be lower.

α = convection coefficient	7.7	[W/m²K]
A = surface	1	[m²]
T_s = surface temperature	80	[°C]
T_a = air temperature	20	[°C]
Q = heat current by convection	462	[W]

TRANSMISSION

Heat can be transferred through a material by transmission (5.9). The size of the heat current that is generated by heat transmission depends on the heat transmittance properties of the material. The higher the thermal transmittance coefficient (λ), the higher the heat current allowed to pass through the material. A single membrane is not able to keep heat outside or inside the building because of its lack of thickness. The thermal transmittance coefficient of the membranes of ETFE cushions is relatively high compared to the encapsulated air.

$Q = A \cdot (\lambda / d) \cdot (T_2 - T_1)$	[W]
Q = heat current by transmission	[W]
A = surface	[m^2]
λ = transmission coefficient	[W/mK]
d = thickness	[m]
T_2 = outside surface temperature	[°C]
T_1 = outside surface temperature	[°C]

5.9 ————————————

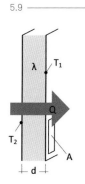

$Q = A \cdot (\lambda/d) \cdot (T_2 - T_1)$

Heat transfer by transmission.

Example

The heat transmission through the construction can be visualised as a series of resistances. The external resistance is 0.04 m^{2}K/W, the internal resistance is 0.13 m^{2}K/W and the resistance of a cavity of approximately 5 cm with standing air is 0.17 m^{2}K/W. The thermal transmittance coefficient (λ) of PVC is 0.15 W/m^{2}K. The thermal resistance of one membrane, with a thickness of 1 mm, is 0.001 / 0.15 = 6.67 · 10^{-3} m^{2}K/W. The scale between the thermal resistances of the membrane and the standing air inside the cavity is 6.67 · 10^{-3} : 0.17 or 1 : 25. It can be concluded that a single membrane does not have a high thermal resistance compared to the thermal resistance of the air cavity.

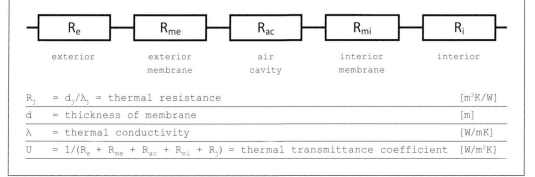

R_e	R_{me}	R_{ac}	R_{mi}	R_i
exterior	exterior membrane	air cavity	interior membrane	interior

R_j	= d_j/λ_j = thermal resistance	[m^{2}K/W]
d	= thickness of membrane	[m]
λ	= thermal conductivity	[W/mK]
U	= $1/(R_e + R_{me} + R_{ac} + R_{mi} + R_j)$ = thermal transmittance coefficient	[W/m^{2}K]

In order to clarify the relation between the different heat transfer processes (radiation, convection, transmission), an example is provided of a non-transparent single-layer membrane façade construction. The conditions in the summer in the Netherlands result in a temperature difference along the façade of 10K: outside temperature 30°C and inside temperature 20°C.

Radiation
The mean total solar radiation on a vertical surface in summer in the Netherlands is approximately 400 W/m².

Radiation of the surface of the façade can be calculated with the Stefan-Bolzmann law.

$E_T = \varepsilon_\lambda \cdot \sigma \cdot T^4$		$[W/m^2]$
ε_λ	= emission coefficient for wavelength λ = approx. 0.90	$[-]$
σ	= Stefan-Boltzmann's constant = $5.669 \cdot 10^{-8}$	$[W/m^2K^4]$
T	= temperature	$[K]$

A surface with temperatures of 10°C, 20°C and 60°C respectively emits 328 W/m², 376 W/m² and 430 W/m².

Convection
Considering a temperature difference of 60K between the air temperature inside and the temperature of the membrane on the surface, the heat flow by convection is 462 W/m². A temperature difference of 10 K will result in 77 W/m².

Transmission
The thermal resistance of the double-layer façade is approximately 0.34 m²K/W. The temperature difference along the construction is 10 K, resulting in a heat current by transmission of approximately 29 W/m².

Conclusion
It can be concluded that façade design preference will be given to a low heat transmittance and a high visible light transmittance. As solar radiation is the most important factor in the physical mechanisms of the façade. It needs to be blocked to prevent internal overheating in the summer.

The infrared part of the solar spectrum causes the greatest amount of heat, consequently, it is this part of the spectrum that should be blocked. The visible light transmittance depends on the degree of transparency of the construction, much desired where transparency in façade construction is sought after.

MEMBRANE FAÇADE CATEGORIES

5.10

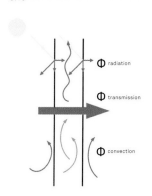

Heat transfer principles and construction.

Membrane façade constructions have important properties that impact the physical function of the spaces they enclose, in relation to the three main heat transfer principles (5.10) discussed on the preceding pages. They can be categorised as follows:

DOUBLE-LAYER CONSTRUCTION
A construction made of two layers with a cavity containing standing air in-between. The standing air leads to a lower heat transfer through transmission. The cavity can also be ventilated in order to further control energy flows.

TRANSPARENT MEMBRANES
Transparent membranes allow for visible light and infrared light to pass through at a high rate. When applying a transparent membrane on the outside of the construction, the internal heat generated in the façade construction by solar radiation must be taken into account. When a transparent membrane is applied on the inside of the building, the internal heat production when sunlight hits construction elements, such as the floor and walls, must be taken into account.

NON-TRANSPARENT MEMBRANES
Non-transparent membranes block direct sunlight and can, therefore, be used as sunscreens. When used on the outside, they prevent sunlight from entering the construction. At the same time, they absorb sunlight and gain warmth but no passive solar heating on the inside of the building results. However, when using a non-transparent membrane on the inside of the construction, the energy-emitting properties of the membrane must be taken into consideration because the membrane will warm up as a result of solar irradiation.

SEMI-TRANSPARENT CONSTRUCTION
The problem with regard to a semi transparent construction is that direct solar radiation causes internal heating. With a solar transmission of 10% in the summer in the Netherlands $100\ W/m^2$ will directly enter the building causing possible overheating.

AIRTIGHT MEMBRANES

Airtight membranes are impenetrable for air. The airflow through the construction is reduced.

AIR-OPEN MEMBRANES

Air open membranes allow air to move freely. They are used as a windbreaker and as solar shading. Outside air can enter the air cavity.

VENTILATED CAVITY

A ventilated cavity has a forced airflow between the inner and outer layer. This airflow is created with a mechanical installation or by temperature or pressure differences along the construction. The airflow is used to minimise the internal heat production by solar irradiation or to obtain hot air for heating the building by passive solar heat gain.

EXAMPLES OF TECHNICAL TEXTILE APPLICATIONS

SECOND-SKIN FAÇADE

In the case of second-skin façades, the textile surface is on the exterior of the building. A ventilated space is created between the textile surface and the façade itself. The textile structure is used for sun protection and is an important element for the overall appearance of the building. The external textile surface can be single-layered, multi-layered (cushions) and insulated.

CLIMATE FAÇADE

Behind the curtain-wall façade a second textile surface is applied. The textile surface is used for sun protection in combination with installations to control the climate of the building.

ROOFS

There are many examples of textile roofs for permanent buildings using single-layered, multi-layered (cushions) and insulated textile structures for sun protection and climate control of the building.

SHELTERS

The climate control of non-permanent or semi-permanent buildings and pavilions depends on the type of construction: pre-stressed membranes and inflatables.

TYPOLOGY OF BUILDING CONSTRUCTIONS

The different methods of climate control with regard to membrane constructions can be divided into four categories:

- transparent membranes on the inside of the construction;
- non-transparent membranes on the inside of the construction;
- transparent membranes on the outside of the construction;
- non-transparent membranes on the outside of the construction.

Additional membrane properties result in air-open, airtight membrane constructions, with or without ventilation.

TRANSPARENT MEMBRANE ON THE INSIDE

This façade construction type has one or multiple layers with a transparent membrane on the inside of the construction. The transparent membrane can be used as an airtight layer (5.11).

5.11

single-layer membrane

multi-layer membrane

air-open membrane

air-open membrane

transparent membrane

transparent membrane

façade / structure

ventilated

exterior | interior

POSITION	Inside							
TRANSPARENT	Yes							
LAYERS	Single				Multi			
AIR TIGHTNESS	Yes		No		Yes		No	
VENTILATION	Yes	No	Yes	No	Yes	No	Yes	No
PRINCIPLE								

An air-open and transparent membrane provides neither shading nor insulation. It can be used for aesthetic purposes. This applies also to multiple layers of air-open and transparent membranes.

NON-TRANSPARENT MEMBRANE ON THE INSIDE

A non-transparent membrane on the inside of the construction can be used for solar radiation protection (5.12).

5.12

POSITION	Inside							
TRANSPARENT	No							
LAYERS	Single				Multi			
AIR TIGHTNESS	Yes		No		Yes		No	
VENTILATION	Yes	No	Yes	No	Yes	No	Yes	No
PRINCIPLE								

TRANSPARENT MEMBRANE ON THE OUTSIDE

A transparent membrane can be used for façade constructions where a clear view is required (5.13). The use of solar heating is possible, especially combined with ventilation.

5.13

POSITION	Outside							
TRANSPARENT	Yes							
LAYERS	Single				Multi			
AIR TIGHTNESS	Yes		No		Yes		No	
VENTILATION	Yes	No	Yes	No	Yes	No	Yes	No
PRINCIPLE								

As with the former construction types, an air open and transparent membrane, be it single or multi-layer, has no technical function and can not provide either shading or insulation. It serves only aesthetic purposes.

NON-TRANSPARENT MEMBRANE ON THE OUTSIDE

A non-transparent membrane on the outside of the construction prevents the solar radiation from reaching the construction so that less heat is produced internally (5.14).

5.14

POSITION	Outside							
TRANSPARENT	No							
LAYERS	Single				Multi			
AIR TIGHTNESS	Yes		No		Yes		No	
VENTILATION	Yes	No	Yes	No	Yes	No	Yes	No
PRINCIPLE								

5.15, 5.16

Pilot project Boogstal for dairy cattle in Dieteren, the Netherlands.

CASE STUDY

The following example is part of a research project in building physics by the Product Development Research Group at the Department of Architecture, Building and Planning (ABP) at Eindhoven University of Technology, the Netherlands. It demonstrates the physical properties and passive climate control qualities of a membrane façade construction. At Eindhoven University of Technology a low-cost and flexible building system for dairy cattle has been developed in cooperation with a coalition of leading consultancy companies [Gijsbers, 2005]. The Boogstal (Arched Stable) was created within the SlimBouwen© approach for building technology and product development [Lichtenberg, 2005] and introduced as a pilot project in 2006 in Dieteren in the south of the Netherlands. The building has been developed to deliver a stable indoor climate of 0°C to 20°C, which is the thermoneutral zone for dairy cattle (5.15, 5.16).

Roof detail: truss struc-
ture, upper and lower
membrane and ventila-
tion openings.

The construction consists of a series of steel truss arches. Between each two adjacent arches a double-layered membrane serves as roof covering and also to create a natural ventilation system which can be adjusted depending on the amount of ventilation needed (5.17).

The roof is primarily designed to keep the indoor temperature low in case of high outdoor temperatures. Dairy cattle are able to withstand cold temperatures easily; therefore, the building is not insulated. By contrast, dairy cattle are highly sensitive to temperatures above 25°C, which causes heat stress and lowers the production of milk drastically.

The double-layered roof consists of an outer layer of 55% open windbreak mesh which tempers the wind speed, but more importantly blocks the major part of sun radiation. Subsequently, part of the collected heat in the membranes is dissipated by the air buffer between the two layers because of convection. Heat from inside the building can get out through the many ventilation openings by buoyancy-induced flow (stack effect) and because of air movement at wind speeds over 3 m/s (5.18).

5.18

Roof detail: a windbreak
mesh on top and a semi-
transparent foil below.

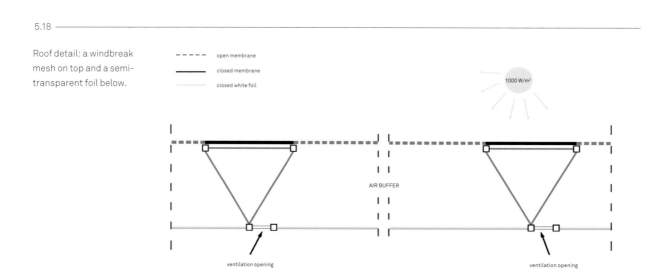

The lower layer of white foil keeps the rain out. Underneath the truss elements, which are closed on top, small open strips for ventilation have been attached, which cover the total length of the structural arc. This results in a homogenous and sufficient ventilation flow through the building, avoiding condensation and providing stable of indoor temperature and humidity levels, as verified during the one-year monitoring phase [Gijsbers et al. 2007]. The white foil prevents direct sunlight from entering the indoor space and creates a diffuse and natural transmission of daylight. As a result, the light intensity achieved is generally comparable to outside conditions on a cloudy day all year round, which is an enormous improvement on indoor comfort compared to traditional housing for dairy cattle. In comparison, for a normal single-layered roof without insulation (for example sheets of corrugated iron, Fibre-cement corrugated sheeting or a single layer of foil), there is approximately 75% less heat flow in the inside of the building during a sunny day (T_a = 30°C; sun load = 1000 W/m²). The surface temperature of the roofing material is also significantly lower: 85°C with a single-layered roof and 35°C with a double-layered roof. These figures result in a large increase of indoor comfort during hot outdoor temperatures.

Cox, M.D.G.M.; Gijsbers, R.; Haas, T.C.A. de, "Applied Design of an Energy-Efficient Multi-Layered Membrane Roofing System for Climate-Control of Semi-Permanent Shelters", in: Kenny, P. et al. (ed.), Proceedings of the 25th PLEA International Conference on Passive and Low Energy Architecture, 22-24 October 2008, University College Dublin, 2008.

Haas, T.C.A. de, Boogstal voor de varkenshouderij – Graduation Report, Eindhoven University of Technology, 2008.

Knoll, W.H.; Wagenaar, E.J.; van Weele, A.M., Handboek installatietechniek, Rotterdam, Stichting ISSO, 2002.

Lichtenberg, J.J.N., Slim-bouwen®, Boxtel, Æneas, 2005.

Pronk, A.D.C.; Haas, T.C.A. de; Cox, M.G.D.M., "Heat-Adapting Membrane", in: Proceedings of Structural Membranes 2007 Conference, Barcelona, 2007.

by ANAIS MISSAKIAN,
KHIPRA NICHOLS
and LILIANE WONG

FROM RAW MATERIAL TO THE FINISHED PRODUCT: INTERIOR TEXTILES

Technical textiles are distinguished by their performance or functional properties, rather than their aesthetic and decorative ones. The distinction between the aesthetic and the functional reflects a century of major developments in the field of textiles. Fuelled by dramatic technological advancements, the modern textile and its characteristics have led to equally dramatic and innovative uses in the interior environment. More recently, the field of nanotechnology has led to hitherto unknown possibilities in the application of textiles. With great promise of future potential that expands the performance capabilities of textiles its role in the interior environment will reach new heights, extending its domain well beyond the drawing rooms of history and the modern office to the interiors of emergency rooms and space capsules.

The historic use of textiles in the interior environment is most significant in the forms of drapery, tapestries, carpets and upholstery. While these applications served the simple and timeless functions of providing warmth, privacy and protection from solar gain, they were selected primarily for their aesthetics. Subsequent developments in fibre content, weaving technology and chemical treatments have improved the functional qualities of textiles, transformed their performance capabilities and enabled them to transcend their decorative role. The path to becoming "technical textiles", the very name alluding to integration with technology, is distinguished by a spirit of experimentation that led to the discovery of new fibres and novel production processes. These advancements, however, also resulted from an evolution in interdisciplinary pedagogy, one that would ultimately reflect the input of the fields of textiles, product design, science and interior architecture.

Creation of a 100% stainless steel weaving for acoustic panels by Sophie Mallebranche at the Museum of Nature and Hunting, Hotel de Guénégaud des Brosses, Paris, France. Specifiers: Jouve-Sazerat Vignaud Architectes.

Aramid fabric.

FIBRE DEVELOPMENT

The spirit of experimentation defines the development of the age-old art of textiles both in enhancing the capabilities of natural fibres as well as in the creation of new, synthetic ones. Fibres are classified into three main types: natural, synthetic-polymer and natural-polymer. Natural fibres including wool, cotton and silk provide strength, sound absorbency, moisture absorbency, thermal properties, elasticity, dye affinity and reaction to chemicals. Natural fibres such as rayon and metallic are considered man-made because they must be highly processed in order to produce textiles. Metallic textiles are durable, non-flammable, corrosion-resistant and flexible (6.1).

Synthetic fibres are products manufactured from polymer-based materials such as poly-amide (nylon), polyester, acrylic, polypropylene, polyethylene, and fibres of the meta-aramid and poly-aramid groups, a class of strong heat-resistant fibres. Lightweight and flexible, the aramid fibre's greatest feature is its strength. Stronger than fibreglass it is, pound for pound, five times stronger than steel (6.2).

Advancements in fibre and yarn development are ongoing not only for synthetic materials but also for those found in nature. Scientists are studying methods to promote greater production of fibres such as dragline silk spun by spiders, a protein fibre with impressive natural strength and tensile properties.

Pioneered by the research of chemical giants such as Dupont for the military, fibre development is among the most innovative of technological research. Technical textiles originate with particular fibres that are spun and constructed into fabrics with function as their primary requirement. Technical textile characteristics must meet criteria requirements that include strength or tenacity, flexibility, resilience, abrasion resistance, absorbency, flammability, heat sensitivity, chemical reactivity and resistance. Fibre research and development, as well as textile construction techniques and technology are at the forefront of advancements in technical textiles for interior applications.

Technical textiles are usually woven but can also be produced by knitting, felting, lace making, net making, non-woven processes and tufting, or a combination of these processes. Most fabrics are two-dimensional, but an increasing number of three-dimensional woven and knitted technical textile structures are being developed and produced.

Woven fabrics generally consist of two sets of yarns that are interlaced at right angles to each other. The threads that run along the length of the fabrics are known as warp ends while the threads that run from selvedge to selvedge are weft picks. Woven technical textiles are designed to meet the specific requirements of a particular application. Their strength, thickness, extensibility, porosity and durability can be varied and depend on: the weave structure, thread spacing, raw materials, filament or staple, count and twist of yarns. Woven fabrics have the potential for greater strength and stability than any other fabric structure.

While there are many variations of weave structure, most technical fabrics are constructed from simple weaves. The majority are plain weave structures where one warp thread is alternately lifted and lowered across one weft thread. An example of one of many variants is the Leno weave structure, in which paired warp yarns are intertwined in a series of figure of eights, and filling yarn is passed through each of the interstices; the fill yarns are trapped tightly between the twisting warp yarns, giving excellent performance characteristics. Structural superiority is also achieved in triaxial weaving where the structural elements run in three directions. This weaving process provides the flexibility of multiple weaving patterns and/or materials, resulting in a thin, lightweight, uniform and highly efficient product.

Until recently, the Jacquard loom designed by Joseph-Marie Jacquard in 1801, was one of the most important innovations in textile production. The mechanical Jacquard loom utilised a system of punch cards and hooks in which the hooks and needles were guided by the holes in the punch card. Intricate patterns and structures were achieved by employing a number of cards in a sequence, arranged one after the other and/or used repeatedly. The Jacquard loom was revolutionary as a precursor to computer-programmed looms in its ability to follow an algorithm and its capability to store information on punched cards. The first electronic Jacquard loom was introduced in 1983, eliminating the need for repeats and symmetrical designs and allowing almost infinite versatility. Three-dimensional weaving technology, with a dual-directional shedding operation, has recently been developed. The flexibility inherent in this technology allows for experimentation with all types of fibres and fibre combinations in order to weave solid, shell and tubular structures. One such technology is Jacqform, a patented process that integrates Jacquard-woven designs with a product's geometry, producing components with built-in seams that are product-tailored and part-specific (6.3).

6.3 ——————————————————

Jacqform.

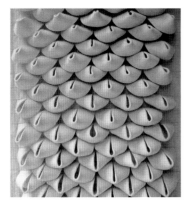

Cut, sewn and finished by
hand, the textiles of Anne
Kyyrö Quinn transform
two-dimensional fabric
into three-dimensional
textures.

A.H.I.T., A Hole in
Textile, lasercut textile
by Camilla Diedrich.

FINISHING

Advancements in science and technology complement those in fibre development in
the transformation of technical textiles. Finishes can add a multitude of performance
capabilities to textiles, including increased durability and water repellence; together with
resistance to shrinkage, wrinkles, creasing, mildew, soil, stains, static and fire. The finishing treatment of a textile is increasingly important, and both fibre and fabric manufacturers
are investing in research and development in this area. To accommodate diverse appear-
ances, designs, textures and performances, finishes have become increasingly versatile
and can be applied at various stages of textile manufacture. The processes vary widely
from high-tech versions of existing treatments, such as coatings and laminates, to printing, embossing, moulding and sculpting, a recent development in which thermoplastic
ultra-microfibres are used to create high-relief surfaces or three-dimensional structures
(6.4, 6.5).

Building upon a starching process commonly used in the 19th century to make stain- and
wrinkle-resistant cloth, soaking fabrics in various solutions is now a common textile finishing process. Since the 1990s, finishing agents have been used to achieve various fabric
characteristics. These possibilities are seemingly limitless, from formaldehyde finishes for
crease resistance to biocidic finishes. Another type of finishing is achieved through lamination, either with a visible polymer membrane or even an invisible one. Visible laminates can
create striking visual effects by using materials that reflect or refract light, or even create
holographic, three-dimensional effects. Invisible laminates can create high-performance
fabrics, such as Gore-Tex, which uses a polytetrafluorethylene (PTFE) layer that is permeable to air while preventing the penetration of water.[1]

A major breakthrough for interior applications is the development of fire-retardant finishes
that comply with global non-flammable classifications. Textiles for indoor use are soaked
in fire-retardant solutions primarily formulated from boric acid and borax. Textiles for outdoor use are soaked with chlorinated paraffin, chlorinated synthetic resins or chlorinated
rubber. The standard for effectiveness of these treatments is determined by the weight
of chemicals remaining after the materials dry. These treatments, however, offer little
resistance against severe fire exposure. As an alternative to post-manufacturing treatments, non-flammable classifications can also be achieved through the use of fibres and
yarns that are permanently flame-retardant. This produces a fabric with flame-retardant
properties firmly anchored in the fibre, where they are not affected by external influences.

In general, there is a shift from finishing fabrics with coatings and laminates, to enhancing fibres on the nano-level, thus enabling them to better serve specific functional requirements. In addition, fabrics are being developed where the yarns and threads are combined with stain-, water- and bacteria-resistant blockers during the weaving process.

In response to increasing demand for environmentally friendly textiles that conserve resources without posing health hazards, tests on finishing additives are underway at a number of commercial laboratories. This work is undertaken in compliance with several international standards. The Oeko-tex Certification standard limits the levels of certain chemicals in textile products. The Bluesign standard places a reliable and proactive tool at the disposal of the entire textile production chain, from raw materials and component suppliers to textile manufacturers, retail and brand companies, and consumers. Other standards include: the Intertek Eco-Certification, the Global Organic Textile Standard (GOTS) and the WRAP (Worldwide Responsible Apparel Production Principles) Certification.

APPLICATIONS IN THE INTERIOR ENVIRONMENT

These developments in fibre and finish have led to enhanced textile attributes that broaden their function in interior environments. Key attributes such as load-bearing capabilities, augmented acoustical properties, UV resistance and light control have inspired new applications.

STRENGTH

Increased strength is a primary factor in the transformation of technical textiles. It has enabled textiles to take on a structural role in which both the fabric membrane and its supporting frame carry loads. Structural fabrics are of a woven cloth base, stabilised and protected by a coating applied on both sides to ensure the integrity of the fibre while giving it flexibility. The structural fabrics most commonly used for interior applications are: laminated or PVC-coated polyester, silicon-coated woven fibreglass and PVC- or PTFE-coated glass cloth. Typical values of tensile strength are between 300 and 1100 daN/5cm depending on the type of fabric.

Tensile forms have the structural integrity to create interior partitions, half-walls and ceilings but also complete rooms. For example, a continuous, curving fabric ribbon made of fire-rated Lycra and installed at the J.S. Bach Chamber Music Hall, functions as wall, half-wall, handrail, ceiling and acoustic reflector, enhancing the acoustics while delineating the various performance spaces (6.6).

J.S. Bach Chamber Music
Hall, Manchester, Great
Britain. Zaha Hadid
Architects.

At the MiNO Hostel in
Migliarino, Italy, tensile
structures serve as
individual rooms. Antonio
Ravalli Architetti.

Comprising textile tensioned around a frame, such structures are self-supporting and in many instances, free-standing (6.7).

As highly tensioned membranes, these forms are not limited to a construction vocabulary of orthogonal components and can assume complex curves and unconventional forms. Complex forms are realised through the use of three-dimensional computational modelling techniques in which fabric, tautly stretched to maximum design loads, is subjected to a series of complementary stresses (6.8, 6.9).

The Cloud Pod and Spiky
Pod seminar rooms in
the Queen Mary Hos-
pital School of Medicine
& Dentistry in London,
Great Britain, are ex-
amples that demonstrate
the possibilities of com-
plex tensile forms.
Will Alsop.

Air-supported or pneumatic structures may be formed from textile membranes. They are tensile structures in which constant air pressure forces the fabric into surfaces of double curvature. These structures are inspired by high-performance applications, originally found outside the building industry, such as inflatable military combat rafts or automotive airbags. Due to the extreme pressure imposed by the air as well as the heavy-duty bonding required at the membrane seams, these structures require textiles woven from reinforced fibres. Fabricated from airtight textile, such structures have the ability to serve as interior standalone elements such as exhibition pavilions and office cubicles (6.10).

Inflatable structures
used as office cubicles,
"Office in a Bucket", by
Inflate Design.

Forms constructed of a single-membrane layer, such as the automotive airbag, rely on the air itself as part of the support (6.11). Pneumatic structures are, in general, lightweight and require less energy for construction and transportation than conventional structures. They are pertinent in adaptive re-usable applications where, as lightweight rooms, they can be easily inserted within the infrastructure of an imperfect host building (6.12).

6.11 ————————————————————————————————————

The Cloud Inflatable
Meeting Room by Monica
Förster depends, in part,
on the air for support.

6.12 ————————————————————————————————————

The MYU Bar designed by
Paul Kaloustian, which
is situated within an old
liquor factory in Beirut,
Lebanon.

ACOUSTICS

When used in dense layers, fabrics have traditionally served an acoustic role by virtue of their intrinsic absorptive qualities. Recent work demonstrates less conventional approaches to designing sound-absorbing surfaces, using not only new materials but re-thinking traditional ones. Utilising natural materials and novel approaches, traditional two-dimensional wool is transformed from its use over flat acoustical panels, to three-dimensional highly absorbent surfaces (6.13, 6.14).

6.13, 6.14 ——————

The work of Anne Kyyrö Quinn's acoustical wall at the Bovis Lend Lease Office in London, Great Britain.

SCI-Arc Auditorium in Los Angeles, USA. A wool ceiling baffle design was created by Hodgetts and Fung Architects.

A further innovative approach to sound absorption uses new textiles that are differentiated from traditional ones by thickness. While such applications formerly required mass (traditional fabric-wrapped acoustic panels are 25-50 mm thick), new textiles, due to the use of synthetic fibres and coatings, can achieve higher levels of sound absorption at thicknesses as small as 0,18 mm. These high-strength, flame-resistant PVC-covered polyester fabrics are perforated with varying aperture sizes and spacings. Such micro-perforated acoustic material absorbs sound by resonance as the micro-perforations convert sound energy into heat. The viscous friction of air passing through the perforations is reinforced by resonance in the volume of air trapped between the material and the rear wall, generating impressive acoustic properties. In such applications, these textiles are often stretched at optimal angles below ceilings and along walls. Absorption rates differ by fabric type and by the depth and content of the plenum behind the fabric.

Technical textiles also have the ability to function as reflective surfaces. The ability to reflect sound and enhance its distribution in a given space is well served by material rigidity provided by the tightness of the woven fibres in combination with fabric coatings such as Teflon or vinyl. Characterised by curvature, tensile structures permit infinite permutations for reflective strategies (6.15).

6.15 ——————

Experimental Media and Performing Arts Center (EMPAC), Rensselaer Polytechnic Institute, Troy, USA. Nicholas Grimshaw.

UV RESISTANCE/LIGHT CONTROL

Today's synthetic textiles have a heightened ability to provide solar protection through the fabric characteristics of solar transmittance, reflectance and absorption. Fabrics commonly used in this application are coated fibreglass and coated glass mesh in which glass fibre yarn is coated with vinyl (PVC) either as individual strands or after it is woven. The composite fabric provides strength and stability in conditions of extreme temperatures, weather and UV exposure. Fabric screens, blinds and shading devices made of these materials can block up to 90%[2] of incoming UV rays while preventing heat loss in the winter. Solar protection devices are common applications for interior spaces enclosed by large areas of glass and skylights (6.16).

6.16 ────────────────────────────────

The sun-tracking device at the Jardine Insurance in London, Great Britain, was enhanced by an integrated intelligent operating system that enables it to rotate with the movement of the sun.

Light control is determined by the fabric's optical values. These include the openness factor, a function of the percentage of openings in the fabric. Visible light transmittance is also determined by the fabric's colour and its visible light reflectance. Through different combinations of these characteristics, the designer can control light levels and produce the desired effects for each interior space and its intended use (6.17, 6.18).

6.17, 6.18 ──

A curved, translucent membrane ceiling provides a diffuse, ethereal atmosphere of introspection at St. Franziskus Church, Regensburg, Germany.

Translucent membrane ceiling panels provide a homogeneous, white light; Brandhorst Museum, Munich, Germany.

A textile's light control function extends beyond the realm of natural light to that of artificial light and its fixtures. Textile ceilings can easily incorporate many types of lighting. While conventional incandescent and fluorescent fixtures are accommodated in generic ceilings, fibre optics and LEDs can be suspended above or even embedded within the textile for special effects and colour (6.19).

The sea floor is projected on and lit from within the textile ceiling; Cabrera Islands National Park Visitors Centre, Spain. Álvaro Planchuelo.

Free-standing textile-wrapped forms containing a light source function as light fixtures and, with the addition of printed graphics, as signage.

FUTURE POTENTIAL

The increased performance potential of textiles has inspired inventive approaches to their use in interiors. The high strength and light weight of new synthetic materials such as carbon fibre have given rise to many uses, from furniture (6.20) to interior partitions. While this spirit of innovation is inspired by the new, its reach also encompasses the old, in re-thinking both means and methodologies. Through simple connection details or high-tech moulding procedures, the traditional piece of fabric may be transformed into a three-dimensional object, resulting in interior elements of rich and unique textures (6.21, 6.22, 6.23).

6.20

The innovative use of carbon fibre in the interior ranges from chairs to walls.

6.21

Three-dimensional soft forms created by the attachment of fabric tiles to each other; Kvadrat Showroom, Copenhagen, Denmark.

Foam and fabric building blocks form walls and provide sound absorption; Kvadrat Showroom, Stockholm, Sweden.

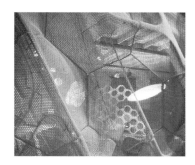

Textiles are three-dimensionally shaped to form lightweight, buttressed combs that can serve as walls and screens.

The technological advancements in the last decades of the 20th century have enhanced the natural attributes of fabrics, resulting in textiles that respond to specific design requirements of today's innovative interior environments. In the 21st century the role of technology has shifted. Once considered a tool, technology is now integrated into and expressed as part of design. In textiles, "fibres, fabrics and textile techniques are becoming seamlessly integrated with technology",[3] providing surfaces that respond to more than one requirement. They are multi-functional with applications across many disciplines. With this blurring of boundaries, in particular between textiles, product design and interior architecture, there is a new future for the role of technical textiles.

This trend began in the late 1990s in the fashion industry with the incorporation of equipment – cameras, microphones and speakers – into clothing. These embedded textiles allowed the wearer of the garment to manually trigger an interface with an information portal. Such innovations inspired an entirely new category of textiles: electronic textiles, or e-textiles, fabrics woven with fibres capable of conducting electrical impulses and transferring information. Conductive fibres and textiles have important applications not only in medical and military fields, but also in engineering and architecture. They are produced by adding different forms of carbon or metals to fibres and yarns, ultimately yielding textiles with electrical properties. Scientists working with nanofibres manipulate atoms and particles to produce fibre as small as 0.001 micrometre. Working with very small units, fibres can be made that have specialised performance characteristics, from improved colour fastness to increased moisture resistance.

Recent developments have also led to the creation of surfaces with a nanolayer coating of "multifaceted molecules [that] enable the fabric to sense and respond to a wide range of conditions it encounters."[4] Through nanotechnology, finishing takes place at the molecular level by permanently attaching nanoscale particles to individual fibres. The use of nanotechnology enables manufacturers to improve functionality, add powerful performance capabilities and use fewer additives, while maintaining the qualities of a fabric. Based on nanoparticle behaviour, this research has increased the potential of fabric finishes, resulting in improved resistance to water, stains, wrinkles, and even to pathogens such as bacteria and fungi.

With the ability to sense and respond through relayed impulses, textiles can now emit light, react to touch or heat, and interact with technology. These e-textiles have greatly broadened the possibilities of technical textiles. While many are in the research or prototype phase they herald future promise for the interior environment, with new functions arising from the seemingly limitless possibilities of fibre development.

With these new possibilities, the attributes of strength, acoustical properties and light control have increased future potential. Enormously strong fibres, such as nickel and silver, heat-resistant para-aramid or plated metal, result in textiles that are, respectively, bullet-proof (Kevlar), resistant to dog bites (Twaron), tear-resistant (Polyment) and have possible applications in high-security environments and heavily trafficked spaces. Glass filaments woven into fabric are able to detect and produce sound, extending well beyond acoustical applications of absorption and sound enhancement. Retro-reflective textiles woven with microscopic glass pellets have the ability to reflect light even in environments with low levels of illumination and have potential applications in windowless or low-light spaces. Fabrics woven with fibre optics, coloured LEDs and electroluminescent wires have the ability to emit and even produce light. They have current applications ranging from light-emitting tapestries (6.24) to glowing furniture slip-covers (6.25) and from light-producing fibre-optic wallpaper (6.26) to fabric woven with LEDs integrating digital imagery and colour.

6.24, 6.25

Woven with fibre optics, Astrid Krogh's electronic textile has the ability to change colours constantly.

Slip-covers of light-emitting textiles; Luminex.

6.26

Luminescent wallpaper lit by fibre optics, designed by Camilla Diedrich.

Touch activates the
panel's colour-changing
properties and allows the
user to leave behind an
imprint.

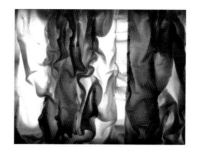

Slow Furl, pioneered by
Ramsgard Thomsen &
Bech, is a responsive
textile system that
reacts to the movement
of the occupant of the
space.

The performance of this future wave of textiles extends well beyond enhanced capabilities to multi-functionality within a broader sphere. Applications are no longer directed only towards issues of spatial function but include ones that range from the emotive to medical diagnosis, from surveillance to energy production. Technical textiles have the ability to capture, but also to make tangible, the human experience within its interior environment. Thermo-sensitive fabrics incorporating colour-changing crystals, for example, allow a user to interact with a textile, bringing a richer sensory experience to interior objects such as walls and furniture (6.27). Pioneers of robotic membranes are experimenting with embedding information technology and digital systems within textiles that can then move, open, close and flow in response to human presence (6.28).

Possibilities also exist for interactive experiences of a different nature, experiences that enhance the human condition. Fabrics with nanoparticle coatings of silver dioxide on nylon yarn or in combination with titanium dioxide result in antimicrobial textiles that are self-cleaning, stain- and odour-resistant, all of which could impact global health. Weaving with electronic modules and electrodes serves a diagnostic function in which textiles have the ability to measure vital signs and transmit such data to different devices ranging from radios and phones to the Internet. Weaving with sensory cilia fibres integrated with radio modules and proximity sensors allows textiles to track movement. Used in hospital rooms or assisted-living housing, these textiles have the ability to react and save lives (6.29).

Using microelectron-
ics, sensors and a radio
module, Sens Floor © by
Future-Shape GmbH is
a flooring system using
intelligent pattern recog-
nition that can detect the
presence, number and
movement of people.

Present developments and the future potential for technical textiles are making a great impact on the interior environment and beyond. In the main performance hall at the Casa da Música in Porto, the solution to a unique acoustical challenge was solved, in part, by layered curtains, each serving a specific function; an acoustic curtain, a blackout curtain, a transparent sun-reflective voile and a "view filter" consisting of a loose mesh of hand-tied knots. Petra Blaisse's curtains have now become synonymous with the project, noted for both its functional and its poetic impact (6.30).

Blaisse notes that the concept of curtain "... was influencing the architecture."[5] This can be seen in recent research that projects future possibilities of technical textiles in conjunction with extreme interfaces. One such project advances the concept of curtains by replacing the façade of a house with a technical textile curtain – a curtain that has the ability to harness solar energy. In so doing, one observes the full transformation of textile from its age-old form of drapery, historically selected for its decorative role, to the highly functional role of a future energy source. In the interior environment, there is promise of a new frontier for the role of technical textiles.

6.30

Petra Blaisse's layered curtains in the main auditorium of the Casa da Música by OMA in Porto, Portugal.

Special thanks to research assistant Patricia Lomando.

1   Braddock Clarke, S. and O'Mahony, M., Techno Textiles 2: Revolutionary Fabrics for Fashion and Design, London, Thames and Hudson, 2007.

2   Products such as the Mermet product E-Screen provides up to 90%, while those like the Koch Membrane PVC/pes product provides up to 75%.

3   Quinn, B.: Textile Futures: Fashion, Design and Technology, New York, Berg Publishing, 2010, p. 5.

4   Ibid., p. 70.

5   McGuirk, J. and Blaisse, P.: ICONEYE Icon Magazine Online, ICON 038, August 2006.

by ROLF H. LUCHSINGER

THE NEW LIGHTWEIGHT STRUCTURE: TENSAIRITY

INTRODUCTION

Technical textiles have been used in architecture and construction for many decades. With the realisation of large buildings with roof structures and claddings made of high-tech fabrics, technical textiles have gained increasing importance and are sometimes called the sixth building material next to stone, wood, steel, concrete and glass. One of the reasons to use fabrics in large structures is their light weight. Fabrics operate completely under tension, which is the most efficient way for a structure to carry loads. The widespread use of technical textiles in architecture and construction has mainly been possible due to improvements in fibre material properties, paralleled by improvements in computational techniques. Indeed, the price for saving weight with a fabric structure is a more involved design and construction procedure that relies on the power of today's computers.

Among fabric structures, pneumatic structures have always played a special role.[1-3] They are used as air-houses for seasonal coverings, e.g. of tennis courts (7.1), and as beam elements for special applications. These so-called air-beams have found, here and there, a niche, e.g. as tents (7.2) or structures for advertisements (7.3). In 1996 the company Festo presented, an air-beam-based hall called "airtecture".[4] These ephemeral applications take advantage of the most prominent properties of pneumatic structures such as compact transport and storage volume, fast and easy set-up, as well as low weight. Nevertheless, the potential application of air-beams in architecture and civil engineering is very limited; the main reason being their very poor load-bearing capacity. The fabric of the air-beam can only support compressive forces up to its level of pre-stress, as given by the air pressure.

The air-house as an example of an air-supported structure. The whole volume is filled with air under very low pressure.

Air-beams as primary structural elements for small tents.

Air-beam as primary structural element for advertisement purposes.

Even a relatively high air-pressure of 1 bar (10^5 N/m^2) is still three orders of magnitude smaller than the yield strength of a metal such as steel. Thus, air-beams operate in a different load and deflection category compared to conventional structures and can only be used when large deformations, even for very moderate loads, are tolerable. It is tempting to increase the load capacity of air-beams by applying a very high air pressure. However, a high air pressure leads to high tensional stresses in the fabric structure that can only be resisted by expensive fibres with high tensile strength. Furthermore, the stored energy in the beam increases, raising severe safety and air tightness issues. Therefore, highly pressurised air-beams are only feasible for dedicated applications such as army shelters,[5] and cannot be considered as a valuable solution for civil architecture.

It is the goal of the new structural concept Tensairity[6] to overcome the load deficiencies of air-beams and thus make inflatable structures useful as primary structures for architecture and civil engineering applications. This article gives an overview of the technology. The basic concept of Tensairity is presented together with a discussion of recent results of ongoing research. Initial applications, e.g. the parking garage in Montreux, are highlighted and conclusions drawn regarding the state of the technology.

THE TECHNOLOGY

The basic concept of Tensairity is to increase the stiffness of an air-beam by the integration of cables and struts. The fundamental beam consists of a cylindrical air-beam, a compression strut tightly connected with the air-beam and two tension cables spiralled around the air-beam and attached at each end to the compression strut (7.4). The compression and tensional forces under bending load are taken by the strut and the cables respectively. The air-beam's role is to direct the load transfer between compression and tension elements, and to stabilise the compression element against buckling.

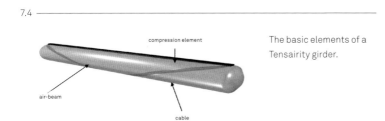

compression element

air-beam

cable

The basic elements of a Tensairity girder.

Simple analytical expressions have been developed for dimensioning the hull, the compression and tension elements for a Tensairity girder under bending load. According to the basic Principles of Tensairity,[7] the bending moment for a given applied load makes it possible to determine the forces in the compression and tension elements. For a homogeneous distributed load q, the force in the tension element T is estimated by

$$T = \frac{q \cdot L \cdot \gamma}{8} \tag{1}$$

with L the span and γ the slenderness of the girder, defined as the ratio of span over diameter. As the cables are connected to the compression element, the tension forces are transferred to the compression element; therefore buckling has to be considered. The compression element is tightly connected with the hull of the air-beam and one can consider the air-beam as an elastic foundation for the compression element; the modulus of the elastic foundation is a function of the air pressure. A simple estimate of the buckling load is given by

$$P = 2 \cdot \sqrt{\pi \cdot p \cdot E \cdot I} \tag{2}$$

with p the air pressure and $E \cdot I$ the bending stiffness of the compression element. Thus, for a given pressure, the bending stiffness of the compression element can be determined in order that the buckling load capacity is higher than the compressive load transmitted by the cables (Equation 1). Typical air pressure values for Tensairity girders with distributed loads are of the order of 100 mbar.

Properties of the
synergetic structure
Tensaririty.

Tensairity

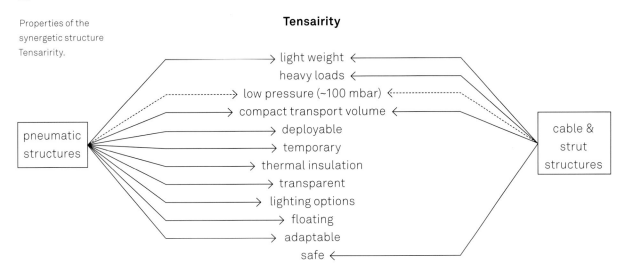

The hoop tension force in the hull of the air-beam *n* is given by

$$n = p \cdot R \tag{3}$$

with *R* the radius of the hull; to a good approximation, n is independent of the applied load. Equations 1, 2 and 3 allow for a first dimensioning of the compression and tension element as well as of the hull of a Tensairity girder, and have proven to be reliable for the many structures built during the last few years.

Shapes of Tensairity girders other than cylindrical have been considered. It was found that the spindle shape leads in general to stiffer structures.[8,9] In consequence this has become the most commonly used shape. Another important finding is that the air pressure is determined by the load per area and is independent of the span and slenderness of a Tensairity structure. This is interesting especially when wide-span structures are considered. The name Tensairity derives from a combination of tension, air and integrity, or alternatively, the combination of tensegrity and air.[10]

The alliance of flexibility and stiffness, of weakness and strength in Tensairity leads to a multitude of interesting properties (7.5). Each property can be related to the underlying air-beam or cable-strut structure. Light weight and small transport volume are properties of both the pneumatic structure and the cable-strut structure. The capacity to carry heavy loads is ensured by the cable-strut structure, while fast set-up, the temporary nature, thermal insulation, lighting options, the floating option and adaptivity, have their roots in the pneumatic structure. The low air pressure is an emergent property of the combination of both structures. It is the sum of all these properties that make Tensairity such a unique structure and ideal applications are always those that benefit from several of them. A number of permanent Tensairity structures such as roof structures and a bridge have been realised so far (see "Realised structures" later in this chapter). Tensairity is also very well suited for temporary applications given its low weight, compact transport volume, the option for fast and easy set-up, all combined with a high load-bearing capacity.

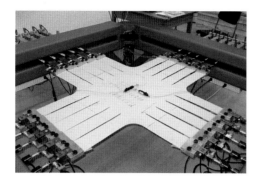

Biaxial tension machine at Empa for the determining of the mechanical properties of fabrics.

RESEARCH AND DEVELOPMENT

Tensairity's combination of materials and components having completely different properties – low air pressure, fabric hulls, cables and struts – leads to an involved structural system. Simultaneous research and development were essential to understanding the structural behaviour, the strengths and limitations of the concept, as well as for further improvement of the system. The ultimate goal is for the technology to be widely used and applied by engineers. Thus, simple formulas for the fast pre-design of Tensairity structures, numerical calculation methods and application guidelines are important. To this end, spindle-shaped girders were studied under local bending loads[9,11] and distributed loads[9,12] using a test rig (7.7). The investigation of Tensairity columns under axial compression (7.8) revealed that their stiffness and load-bearing capacity are comparable to those of a conventional truss structure.[13,14] An analytical model based on a circular arch supported by an elastic foundation was able to predict the axial stiffness of the column, although an analytical model to determine the buckling load has not yet been established.

While some of the basic features of Tensairity structures can be reasonably approximated with simple analytical models, the detailed structural behaviour requires study using numerical methods. Finite Element Method (FEM) calculations have proven to be an important tool for this task.[8] FEM predictions were compared to experimental results for a spindle-shaped girder under bending load. [9,11] The forces in the compression and tension element as well as the displacement of the compression element were accurately determined, although a significantly lower deflection was predicted at the tension side compared to the measured value. This difference was attributed to an over-simplification when modelling the fabric hull material. For simplicity this was modelled as being linear isotropic whereas in reality fabrics behave in a non-linear orthotropic manner. In order to measure the Young's modulus, the Poisson's ratio and the shear modulus, biaxial tensile tests with various load ratios need to be undertaken. Such biaxial tests are currently under way on PVC-coated polyester fabrics, using a purpose-built machine recently installed at the Center for Synergetic Structures at Empa, the Swiss Federal Laboratories for Materials Science and Technology (7.6). To improve the estimation of fabric properties for FEM modelling, a simple and computationally efficient non-linear orthotropic fabric model has been developed.[15] The major goal of this line of research is to scrutinise the role of the fabric in Tensairity structures.

Test rig at Empa for investigating spindle-shaped Tensairity beams under bending load.

Test rig at Empa for the investigating of the axial stiffness of Tensairity columns.

Alongside fundamental research, further development of this new technology is an important task for the Center for Synergetic Structures. To illustrate the potential of Tensairity for temporary applications, a demonstration 8 m span bridge was recently built and featured in a television programme.[9, 16] The two girders of the bridge were sufficiently compact (7.9) that they could be easily stowed in the boot of a car. Each girder weighed less than 70 kg and was assembled in under 30 min by two people who then carried and positioned them. Finally the car drove over the bridge (7.10), giving an elegant demonstration of the four most important properties of Tensairity: compact size, fast and simple set-up, lightweight and high load-bearing capacity.

A further development was a transparent Tensairity girder (7.11). As the tensile strength of currently available transparent foil is limited, a cable net is used to reduce the tensile stress resulting from the air pressure. The cables of the net are so thin that they have little impact on the structure's transparency. The relative stiffness of the cable with respect to the transparent fabric produces an appealing "bubble wrap" surface to the structure. Interestingly, stabilisation by such equilibrium net configurations is also commonly found in nature and hence gives the structure a somewhat organic appearance. An inflated lamp prototype was also built which highlights this peculiar surface structure (7.12). In another project, in collaboration with the Vrije Universiteit Brussels, deployable Tensairity structures are being investigated.[17] The goal is to develop Tensairity structures that can be set up without assembly and solely by inflation, as with conventional pneumatic structures. The potential of Tensairity for inflated wing structures is also being studied.[18]

7.9

A single girder of the demonstration car bridge with 8 m span in the dismantled state.

7.11

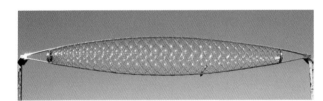

Transparent Tensairity girder reinforced with a cable net.

7.10

Demonstration of the load-bearing capacity of the Tensairity car bridge in a TV-show.

 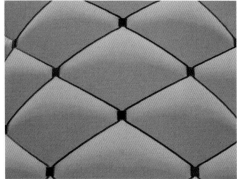

Inflated lamp.

REALISED STRUCTURES

In recent years, several initial applications of Tensairity have been realised, mainly in the field of civil engineering. The driving force behind all these applications is the Swiss company Airlight, responsible for their engineering. Possibly the most impressive one to date is the parking garage roof in Montreux, Switzerland, conceived by Luscher Architectes in 2004.[19] This membrane roof is supported by 12 spindle-shaped Tensairity girders with spans of up to 28 m (7.13). Steel has been used for the upper and lower chord of the Tensairity girder. The same silicon-coated glass fibre fabric is used for the covering membrane as well as for the Tensairity girders. The air pressure in the girders is about 100 mbar. The architects have made extensive use of the beams' intriguing lighting possibilities (7.14–7. 17). Variable colour spotlights are mounted at each end of the Tensairity beams. The light shines into the pneumatic structure through translucent end plates, illuminating the girders internally in a surprisingly homogeneous fashion. The colour of each beam can be controlled by software and dynamically changed to provide vibrant lighting possibilities.

7.13

Tensairity roof structure with up to 28 m span for a parking garage in Montreux, Switzerland, Luscher Architectes SA & Airlight Ltd., 2004.

Illumination of the roof structure at night.

Tensairity bridge with 52 m span in Lanslevillard, France, Charpente Concept SA, Barbeyer Architect & Airlight Ltd., 2005.

A 52 m bridge at a ski resort in the French Alps, supported by two asymmetric spindle-shaped Tensairity girders, was completed in 2005 (7.18) and is, to date, the largest structure of its type. In the winter, a ski slope runs over the bridge and the deck is covered with a thick layer of snow giving rise to high loads. Outside the winter season it is used as a pedestrian bridge. The compression element of the structure is made of wood while the tension element is made of steel. This bridge is an impressive demonstration of the potential of Tensairity for heavily loaded wide-span structures.

Tensairity canopy in Pieterlen, Switzerland, Airlight Ltd., 2005.

View inside the canopy.

While the examples shown rely on Tensairity beams, the concept can also be used for shell-like structures. An example for this approach is a canopy in Pieterlen, Switzerland (7.19). Two grids of steel profiles form the upper and lower layer of the structure. The grids of the two layers are connected by tension elements in order to preserve the thickness of the structure under inflation. An upper and lower fabric layer keeps the structure airtight. The air pressure pre-tensions the fabric and stabilises the two metal grids. As there is essentially only air inside the structure, light is used to enhance the optical appearance

Tensairity advertisement pillar with 20 m height, Airlight Ltd., 2004.

Exhibition stand with Tensairity elements, Breitling SA & Airlight Ltd., 2004.

of the canopy at night. It is possible to look through the structure via a window, from the stairs inside the building. Figure 7.20 shows the tension connections between the upper and lower layer as well as the fabric bulging between the steel grid.

A realised temporary application of Tensairity is an advertisement pillar (7.21). The prototype had a height of 20 m and could withstand wind speeds up to 100 km/h without any bracing. These advertisement pillars can be used for mobile marketing, e.g. at fairs, open-air festivals or sport events. A further temporary application was demonstrated in an exhibition stand for a Swiss watch manufacturer. Four cylindrical Tensairity girders provided the structural support to a hanging platform where a sports car was exhibited to visitors (7.22).

CONCLUSION

Pneumatic structures are a special type of fabric structure with interesting properties. The hybrid Tensairity concept overcomes the strength deficiencies of pneumatic structures and thus opens up new options for technical textiles in architecture and engineering. Ongoing research and development are leading to a better understanding of the system's structural behaviour while revealing new applications. A number of initial projects, mainly architectural, demonstrate the feasibility of the technology in terms of cost, safety and structural integrity. The know-why and know-how increase with every project undertaken. This is especially true for the detailing, which is of great importance for this type of structure. The underlying strengths of Tensairity – conceptual simplicity, synergetic interactions leading to enhanced structural behaviour, the efficient use of different materials, its suitability for temporary structures – are all becoming increasingly important in today's global, fast-growing, fast-moving world. It will be interesting to see what place this technology will find in it.

1 Topham, S., Blow up: inflatable art, architecture and design, Munich, Prestel Verlag, 2002.

2 Otto, F.; Trostel, R., Zug-beanspruchte Konstruktionen" Frankfurt, Ullstein Fachverlag, 1962.

3 Herzog, T,; Minke, G.; Eggers, H., Pneumatische Konstruktionen, Stuttgart, Gerd Hatje, 1976.

4 Schock, H.-J., Soft Shells. Design and technology of tensile architecture, Basel, Birkhäuser Verlag, 1997; p. 102-105.

5 Vertigo Inc., www.vertigo-inc.com, 2009.

6 The Tensairity technology was developed by the company Airlight Ltd. in close collaboration with the firm Prospective Concepts AG. Recently, the Tensairity activities of Prospective Concepts AG were transferred to the Center for Synergetic Structures, a public private partnership between Empa and Festo. The main objective of the Center is to strengthen the R&D of synergetic structures, especially of Tensairity structures.

7 Luchsinger, R.H.; Pedretti, A.; Steingruber, P.; Pedretti, M., "The new structural concept Tensairity: "Basic principles", in: Zingoni, A. (ed.), Proceedings of the Second International Conference on Structural Engineering, Mechanics and Computationg, Lisse, Balkema / Zeitlinger, 2004, p. 323-328.

8 Pedretti, A.; Steingruber, P.; Pedretti, M.; Luchsinger, R.H., "The new structural concept Tensairity: FE-modeling and applications", in: Zingoni, A. (ed.), Proceedings of the Second International Conference on Structural Engineering, Mechanics and Computation, Lisse, Balkema / Zeitlinger, 2004, p. 329-333.

9 Luchsinger, R.H.; Sydow, A.; Crettol, R., "Structural behavior of asymmetric spindle-shaped Tensairity girders under bending loads", Thin-Walled Structures 49 (9), 2011, p. 1045-1194.

10 Luchsinger, R.H.; Pedretti, A.; Steingruber, P.; Pedretti, M., Light weight structures with Tensairity, in Motro, R. (ed.), Shell and Spatial Structures from Models to Realizations, Montpellier, Éditions de l'Espérou, 2004.

11 Luchsinger, R.H.; Crettol, R., "Experimental and numerical study of spindle shaped Tensairity girders", International Journal of Space Structure 21(3), 2006, p. 119-130.

12 Teutsch, U., Tragverhalten von Tensairity-Trägern, Zurich, vdf Hochschulverlag, 2011.

13 Plagianakos, T.S.; Teutsch, U.; Crettol, R.; Luchsinger, R.H., "Static response of a spindle-shaped Tensairity column to axial compression", Engineering Structures 31, 2009, p. 1822-1831.

14 Wever, T.E.; Plagianakos, T.S.; Luchsinger, R.H.; Marti, P., "Effect of fabric webs on the static response of spindle-shaped Tensairity columns", Journal of Structural Engineering 136(4), 2010, p. 410-418.

15 Galliot, C.; Luchsinger, R.H., "A simple model describing the non-linear biaxial tensile behavior of PVC-coated polyester fabrics for use in finite element analysis", Composite Structures 90(4), 2009, p. 438-447.

16 Luchsinger, R.H.; Crettol, R.; Plagianakos, T.S., "Temporary structures with Tensairity", in: International Symposium IASS-SLTE 2008, 3rd Latin American Symposium on Tensile-Structures, Acapulco, 2008.

17 De Laet, L.; Luchsinger, R.H.; Crettol, R.; Mollaert, M.; De Temmermann, N., "Deployable Tensairity structures", Journal of the International Association for Shell and Spatial Structures 50(2), 2009, p. 121-128.

18 Breuer, J.M.C.; Luchsinger, R.H., "Inflatable kites using the concept of Tensairity", Aerospace Science and Technology 14(8), 2010, p. 557-563.

19 Pedretti, M.; Luscher, R., "Tensairity-Patent – Eine pneumatische Tenso-Struktur", Stahlbau 76(5), 2007, p. 314-319.

ARCHITECTURAL TEXTILES

SEINE-AVAL WATER PURIFICATION PLANT

Location:
Achères, France
Building type:
Enclosures for water
filtration tanks
Client: SIAAP
Architects: Adrien
Fainsilber and AAE,
Fribourg, Switzerland
(Jean-Michel Capeille)
Membrane/metalwork
design: ARCORA,
Arcueil, France

Contractor for fabrica-
tion and installation:
Esmery Caron Struc-
tures, Dreux, France;
Project manager:
Philippe Bariteau
Membrane type:
Woven polyester fibre,
formulated vinyl/PVDF
coating on both sides
Membrane area:
17,300 m²
Completion: 2006

Following the successful use of technical textiles for covering the upstream water treatment plant at Valenton, a similar approach has been adopted for the downstream nitrate treatment plant at Achères.

The Achères site is the largest water treatment plant serving the Paris region and one of the largest in Europe. Approximately 1,700,000 cubic metres of wastewater are treated daily. This case study concerns the tensioned textile membrane structures (1) enclosing the 84 Biosty filtration tanks.

The tanks contain the wastewater during the final stages of treatment before it is released back into the river Seine. The Biosty process, which results in the removal of nitrogen compounds and the return of nitrogen gas to the atmosphere, requires that the tank surfaces receive good natural ventilation. Further requirements are that the tank surface be shaded from the sun to avoid unwanted algae growth, and in addition, can be quickly inspected by technicians as they pass. While satisfying these technical needs, the architect sought an enclosure

design that was both sober yet modern, and one that harmonised well with the surrounding environment.

The chosen technical textile solution not only meets the requirements but was easy to install. Fastening and tensioning the textile membrane panels was undertaken by a team of four installers working from the plant's concrete walkways or from light moveable scaffold towers. Each of the 84 filtration tanks, each measuring 16 by 11 metres in plan, has a separate membrane roof covering. The membrane panels are fixed by lacing them to the stainless steel superstructure (2).

Two different textiles were chosen for the tank enclosures. The largest textile surface was that of the tank roof. This was formed from a tensioned fabric of woven polyester fibre, coated on both sides, with formulated vinyl and then with a finishing varnish coat of PVDF. The membrane is coloured silver grey on one side and blue on the other. The silver grey colour was chosen for the outside to reflect a maximum amount of radiation for the benefit of the treatment process.

Nonetheless, the textile membrane has excellent durability against UV exposure. The second textile was used for the vertical side and spandrel panels. While fabricated from materials and processes similar to the roof membrane textile, this material is lighter in weight and has an open weave, thereby allowing air circulation and adequate transparency for quick visual inspection of the treatment area. Both textiles have the required fire resistance rating.

The water purification site at Achères, constructed according to sustainable development objectives, is dedicated to cleansing and recycling, and not only of wastewater. The pumps that return the purified water to the Seine are powered by "green" electricity, generated from turbines powered by river water. Furthermore, raw materials needed in the treatment processes are transported to the site by river barge to reduce road pollution. The chosen technical textile enclosures not only provide the necessary environment for the treatment processes, while ensuring the site's harmonious integration with its environment, but are made from fully recyclable materials. **rp**

1 – Biostyr tank enclosures.

2 – Membrane fixed by lacing to the superstructure.

3 – Translucent side and spandrel panels.

COLMAR OUTDOOR THEATRE

Location:
Colmar, France
Building type:
Outdoor theatre
General Contractor:
Direction architecture
Ville de Colmar
Engineers, membrane:
ARCORA, Arcueil,
France
Architect and project
manager: Christian
Bignossi

Contractor for fabrica-
tion and installation:
Esmery Caron Struc-
tures, Dreux, France
(Philippe Bariteau);
Everest
Membrane type:
Polymer-coated
polyester fibre
Membrane area:
1,800 m^2
Completion: 2009

Inaugurated at the 62nd Alsace Wine Festival in August 2009, the Colmar outdoor theatre displays its dramatic textile roof (1).

The east and west stands, each protected by a textile membrane 900 m^2 in area and weighing 2.2 tonnes, protect theatregoers from the elements. While the fabric provides diffuse natural light and optimum indoor comfort during the day, as night falls, its translucence adds to the palette of lighting effects.

The textile chosen for this application is a fabric made from woven polyester fibre, coated on both sides by a PVDF polymer. The textile is coated using a patented process that pre-tensions both warp and weft fibres such that the fabric is held flatter, enabling the application of a thicker, more uniform coating. The resultant fabric has greatly enhanced durability through resistance to weathering, soiling and pollution. The textile achieves a minimum 15-year lifespan.

The membrane analysis confirmed higher levels of stress around the central anchorage points, which were therefore reinforced with a double-membrane layer (2). Each roof membrane was designed to span between two high points and multiple corner anchorage plates, the edges of the membrane being stiffened by edge cables in accordance with normal practice.

The two central high points of both roof membranes are fixed to two parallel cables on a single axis (4). The parallel cables are strung between the mastheads of two tubular steel tripod structures, themselves braced by steel guy cables anchored to the ground. The membrane's corner anchorage plates are fixed to shorter masts, similarly anchored to the ground. Installation of the roof structures was completed in three weeks by a team of six to seven operatives.

Aesthetics and multiplicity of forms, lightness and transparency, strength, speed of implementation, sustainability and protection of the environment are all strengths of this technical textile solution.

"This is the first such architectural textile project of this importance mounted on a funicular type cable in France. The technical prowess of this solution lies in the fact that there is no central mast. It is thus all about large spans giving unencumbered space providing visual comfort, while also conveying a structural slenderness to the concept" (3), concludes Philippe Bariteau of Esmery Caron. In spring, summer and autumn, the outdoor theatre can now accommodate spectators and visitors in comfort. **rp**

1 – A most original costume.

2 – Central anchorage stiffening with a double-layer membrane.

3 – No mast equals visual comfort.

4 – Parallel cables on a single axis.

PUERTO MADERO TERRACE

Location: Puerto Madero Docks, Buenos Aires, Argentina
Building type: Roof over restaurant and bar terrace
Structure type: Single-membrane canopy
Client: Private client
Architect: WAGG Soluciones Tensadas, Buenos Aires

Engineer, membrane: WAGG Soluciones Tensadas
Membrane type: Formulated vinyl-coated polyester fibre textile, PVDF finishing varnish
Membrane area: 580 m²
Competition: June 2009

The next case study is located at the historic Puerto Madero Docks of Buenos Aires, where the "Fragata Sarmiento" is moored. The focus falls on two technical textile canopies for sheltering visitors as they pause for refreshment on the terrace in front of the mooring.

The nautical setting invites the use of the masts and rigging supporting this membrane structure. Both blend perfectly with those of the historic frigate and are reflected in the form of the adjacent "Woman's Bridge" designed by Santiago Calatrava (1).

The project entailed creating outside refreshment areas that include two canopies covering seating areas, one for food and the second for a gelato-cafe. The canopies are constructed of textile membranes tensioned across a steel support structure.

The design brief required consideration of the surrounding aesthetic, hence the "nautical language" of masts and sails so clearly evoked by a tensile architecture solution. It was also important not to obstruct the view, and to leave maximum space for the circulation of people and equipment (4).

These requirements are achieved by the use of a tensile textile roof suspended from a primary steel support structure. This comprises two principal masts with a collector cable spanning between them and supporting two suspended central cross-bars. An additional six steel hanging cables from each mast provide support points for the canopy ends, and bracing back to the two cross-bars (2).

The membrane material is a single layer of vinyl coated polyester fibre textile with a finishing PVDF varnish, covering a rectangular zone measuring 10 × 30 metres. It is anchored by fixing points at the ends of the hanging cables and cross-bars, rising to supporting arcs, two of which are hung from the masts and two from the collector cable. The supporting arcs give the membrane its double curvature form and act as slender hanging ribs. All the peripheral end points are anchored to the ground by stiffening cables to resist the uplift forces that can act on the membrane. A masonry service kiosk is located at the centre of the canopy between the two cross-bars. WAGG Soluciones Tensadas was responsible for all membrane development and realisation processes, from the primary conceptual sketches, the structural and membrane calculations, the fabric cutting patterns and anchorage details, through to the installation.

The installation process was an interactive sequence between membrane and structure. The masts were passed through the membrane before achieving their final geometric position, an action that caused the pre-installed collector cable to start raising the membrane. The peripheral masts were then installed and the membrane attached to them at its fixing points. Once all of the peripheral masts and stiffening cables were in position, a mechanical screw ring gave the definitive position for the mast-supported metal arcs and thereby provided final membrane tensioning (3). The approximately rectangular canopy is stabilised at its edges by stiffening cables spanning between the fixing points. These give the structure its final external shape. **rp**

1 – Masts and rigging.

2 – Canopy structure.

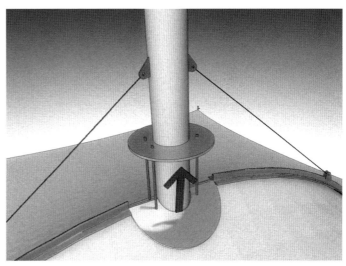

3 – Final membrane tensioning.

4 – Unencumbered space.

OCTAHEDRON

Location: Riyadh, Saudi Arabia
Building type: Mobile publicity display
Structure type: Single-membrane canopy
Client: Private client
Architect: Ali Smaili, King Saud University, Riyadh

Engineer, membrane: Smaili Contracting
Membrane type: Formulated vinyl-coated polyester fibre textile with PVDF finishing varnish
Membrane area: 109 m²
Completion: 2010

Membrane structures have a long history in Saudi Arabia stemming from Bedouin tents, traditionally made of fabric woven from goat hair. Such tent structures remain culturally symbolic and many private houses retain a traditional tent in their inner courtyard; the structure provides a comfortable retreat during the hot summer season.

Recent developments have given rise to radical departures from the traditional Arabian tent structures, with wealthy individuals acquiring "tents" boasting air-conditioning and giant LCD screens. Furthermore today's requirements for sustainability increasingly guide the development and choice of fabrics. In this context it should be remembered that the original goat hair tent fabric was renowned for its ability to adapt to the local climate.

This innovative membrane structure was designed and implemented by a Saudi Arabian company. Designed for a client requiring a striking exhibition structure,

Octahedron succeeds in providing an elegant display area while promoting a structural form that is both modern and culturally relevant. The Octahedron structure (2) was designed to meet the local environmental conditions (wind loads, UV intensity, high temperature).

The shape comprises two opposed cones. From the view of form-finding, the two cones are interlinked. The cable prestress was modified according to the desired form and many form-finding iterations were carried out prior to the selection of the optimum structural shape.

Structurally, the fabric is supported by a central steel column, and at six points: the central mast end points plus four cantilever end points, shared by each cone. A single footing supports the shell structure. In terms of stability, the structure is completely independent of external support. In addition it can be transported with the membrane pre-stressed. The integration between tension and compression, represented by the membrane and mast

respectively, gives a good example of a tensegrity system.

Having selected the final form, an analysis was undertaken with applied loads in order to define the required steel cross sections, the fabric type and the end point detail (3 and 4). The major load factors for fabric and steel design are prestress and wind load. The ASCE code was used to define the C_p (aerodynamic coefficient) value. A wind load of approximately 100 da N/m² was adopted.

The area factor and hence the amount of sunshade obtained can be controlled by providing a foldable mechanism. Modification of the steel support elements (1) would enable a dynamic structure that could open and close according to need.

Conceptually the Octahedron structure can be considered as a typical unit that could form part of a multiple assembly (5). **rp**

1 – The steel support structure.

2 – The constructed canopy.

3 – Stress distribution without and with wind load.

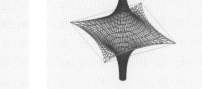

4 – Membrane element stress and deformation with wind load applied.

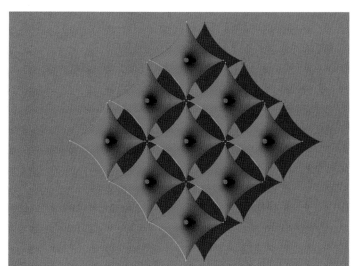

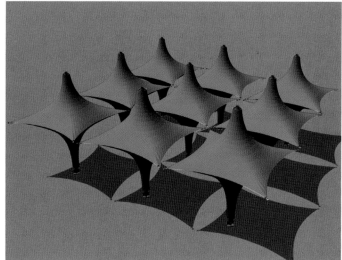

5 – Two views of a bi-directional assembly.

GIANT RUGBY BALL

Location: Paris, France;
London, Great Britain;
Tokyo, Japan;
Sydney, Australia
Building type:
Single-membrane
pneumatic structure
Client: Tourism New
Zealand
Architect: Fabric
Structure Systems Ltd.,
Auckland, New Zealand

Engineer, membrane:
Lindstrand Technolo-
gies, Oswestry, Great
Britain
Membrane type:
Formulated vinyl-
coated polyester fibre
textile, PVDF finishing
varnish to both sides
Membrane area: 832 m²
Completion: 2007

The Giant Rugby Ball is a single-membrane inflated structure, created as a promotional venue for the New Zealand Rugby World Cup in 2011. The structure was designed to be transported from country to country and as a consequence had to satisfy all national construction, health and safety regulations.

The ball's outer skin is held in place by a large oval ring-frame secured to the ground by a heavy water ballast sausage (3). The interior of the ball accommodates 220 people and includes a stage, bar, toilets, storage, control room and seating areas. The Giant Rugby Ball is a proven deployable spatial structure with successful outings to Paris, London, Tokyo and Sydney (1).

Inside the venue the internal surface of the ball is used as a "360-degree" projection surface to promote New Zealand as a destination. The panoramic surround imagery and the structure's particular acoustics give visitors a unique experience (6 and 9).

Visitors enter the ball through an air-lock door designed to maintain the pressure inside the ball. Specialised monitoring equipment maintains a constant air pressure and quality in the ball by controlling two large fans concealed under the floor and the air-conditioning system.

The designers wished to create the image of a ball sitting on a grassed playing field. The position of the plane truncating the ball was chosen in order to attain this image whilst at the same time maximising the internal floor space. After considering several anchorage methods, it was decided to build a raised platform utilising standard scaffold elements with some custom pieces, incorporating a trough lined with plywood around the perimeter (7). This trough carries the PVC water-sausage ballast. The raised platform allows the inflation fans to be mounted under the floor and incorporates the membrane fixing detail at its perimeter.

The ball membrane is made from a woven polyester-based fabric coated with formulated vinyl and finished with an acrylic varnish applied to both sides. An edge bead in the form of a keder-rail strip is bonded to the membrane around its periphery. The keder-rail strip is then retained by an aluminium extrusion attached to the support scaffolding (2). To form the air seal, a plywood deck is first assembled over the scaffold base. This in turn is covered by a shaped PVC membrane extending 50 cm up the inside face of the ball membrane, and also serves as a template for the mezzanine columns and the door location points. Carpet tiles finish the floor and form a wearing layer

to protect the membrane and provide a non-slip floor surface. The ball's outer membrane is continued below the aluminium extrusion to form the skirt and conceal the scaffold base.

In addition to self-weight and dead load, the structural design of the ball considered wind, snow, rain and earthquake loads. Locating the ball in the "shadow" of existing protected structures provides protection against lightning strikes.

Wind load was the most critical. The design wind speed was 23.15 m/s. The shape factors adopted in the design were based on wind-tunnel test data. The ball's design internal pressure was nominally 200 Pa for ordinary conditions and 300 Pa for stormy conditions. Drag and lift forces caused by the wind load are resisted by the weight of the water ballast sausage with a safety factor of at least 1.5.

This venue is managed like any other public venue in terms of safety and emergency, although its unique nature requires particular solutions.

Wind towers with a three-cup anemometer on top are situated at the site location to measure peak wind speed. Procedures are in place for evacuating the people and, when more than 20 m/s peak gusts are predicted, removing the audio-visual and sound equipment, deflating the ball and securing the membrane by roping it to the mezzanine frame (4 and 5).

Smoke alarms and fire-fighting equipment are included; monitoring is undertaken continuously by the audio-visual and sound technicians, who are on duty whenever the venue is open. Japanese regulations required additional fire exits; this was solved by the development of electric heating wires fastened to the membrane that would melt out doorways if required.

Three diesel-powered generators supply the venue, minimising the risk of total power failure. Even with the fans turned off and the doorways open, the occupants have up to 10 minutes to evacuate the structure before air escape allows collapse.

The Giant Rugby Ball has successfully met all design objectives. It is easily transportable and can be erected on site in as little as three days. A number of video sequences showing the erection and travels of the Ball may be found on the Internet. This case study introduces the promotional or entertainment potential for technical textiles, where the structure becomes part of the performance, and in this instance, a veritable saltimbanque. **rp**

1 – From Paris to Sydney.

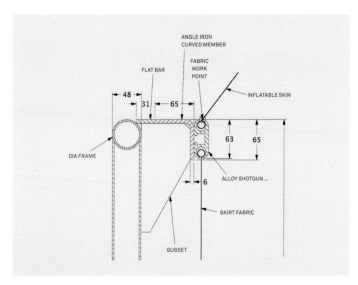

2 – Keder-rail strip and fastening detail.

3 – The ballast tube.

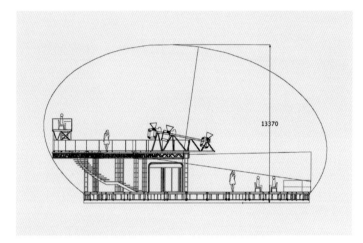

4 – Section and plan.

5 – The mezzanine stairway.

6 – Panoramic projection over the mezzanine level.

7 – The base platform.

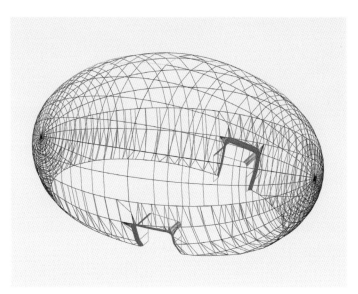

8 – Form-finding.

9 – The panoramic surround imagery and the structure's particular
acoustics give visitors a unique experience.

CENTURY LOTUS STADIUM

Location:
Foshan, China
Building type:
Stadium for track and
field events – stadium
roof, made of a cable
tensioning system
operating from two
metal rings
Client: Foshan City
Council
Architects: GMP,
Hamburg, Germany
Engineer: Schlaich
Bergermann und Part-
ner, Stuttgart, Germany

Contractor: Beijing N&L
Fabric Technology Co.
Ltd., Beijing, China
Membrane type:
Polyester substrate
with vinyl coating and
polyvinylidene flouride
(PVDF) surface treat-
ment
Membrane area:
75,477 m²
Completion: 2007

Foshan was chosen as the venue for the 12th Guangdong Province Sports Meeting, enhancing the cityscape of this South Chinese trade and industry hub on the Pearl River delta, while at the same time adding ultra-modern sports facilities.

The core of the newly planned sports park is the central stadium, whose reflection in the adjacent lake resembles that of a lotus flower, encircled by urban and scenic elements (4). From a distance, the new stadium stands out with its distinctive silhouette and unusual pleated roof structure (5). Made of V-shaped membrane elements, the roof gives the stadium its striking floral form.

The Century Lotus Stadium serves as a venue for football matches and track and field events. It can accommodate 36,000 spectators. The membrane roof covers around 50,000 m² and is the largest cable-tensioned membrane structure in China, with a maximum outer diameter of 310 m and an inner tension ring diameter of 125 m (1). The total length of cable approaches an incredible 36 km.

The roof structure, supported by 40 overhanging concrete cantilever columns, consists of three major sub-structural systems: the outer compression truss, an inner ring of tensioned cable, and the tensioned membrane cladding (2).

The outer compression truss comprises an upper compression ring, lower compression ring and V-shaped diagonals (bracing members). These steel members are welded at joints to form a truss to withstand the vertical and lateral loads. While 1.4 m diameter steel tubes are used for the upper and lower ring, diagonals are made from 1.1 m diameter tubes, which carry not only the vertical force transferred from the upper ring to the bottom, but also the horizontal loads from wind and membrane tensile force. To reinforce the resistance of the lower ring, the steel tubes are supported by cantilevered high-strength concrete columns.

The inner tensioned multi-cable ring serves to anchor and tension upper radial (ridge) cables and lower radial (valley) cables. Each ridge cable is connected to the inner ring through two forked radial cables. The ridge and valley cables are at different elevations and are interconnected by tangential hanger cables (3). The ridge and valley cables, respectively the highest and lowest parts of the roof structure, are important for carrying the load. While gravitational loads, dead load and live load, are supported by the ridge cables, the uplift loads from the wind are resisted by the valley cables. The inner ring comprises ten single cables arranged as two layers of five.

The roof membrane is made up from 80 membrane panels fastened between adjacent radial and valley cables, forming 40 uniform roof units. A durable vinyl-coated polyester fabric was selected as the membrane. The fabric is made using a patented pre-tensioning technology called Précontraint that guarantees dimensional stability and homogeneity, thus ensuring a longer life span. As a result of the surface stability there was virtually no difference between the calculated membrane pre-tensioning and the actual values required for construction. The membrane surface is treated with PVDF to greatly improve soiling resistance. This maintains the appearance of the membrane while ensuring its long lifetime. **rp and ws**

1 – High performance.

2 – The key elements: inner tensioned cable ring, tensioned membrane cladding and steel outer compression truss.

4 – Century Lotus Stadium: technology reflecting the natural world.

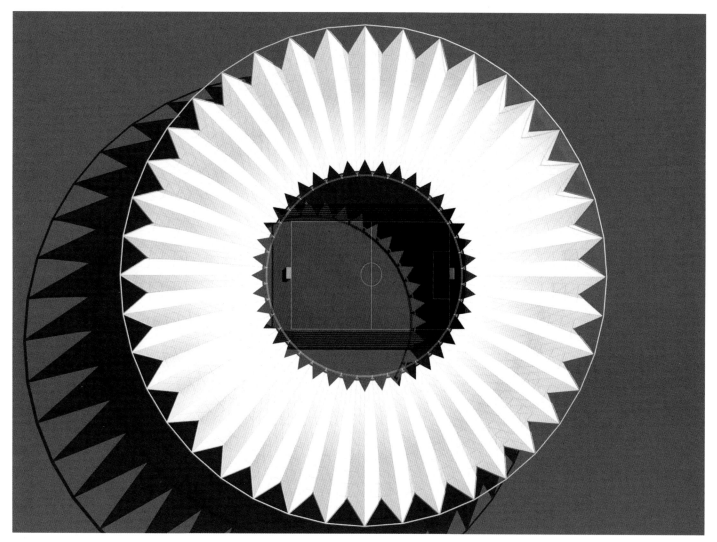

5 – Pleated stadium roof comprising 40 V-shaped membrane units.

OMNILIFE STADIUM

Location: Guadalajara,
Mexico
Building type:
Soccer stadium
Client: Chivas de Gua-
dalajara/Jorge Vergara
Architects: Massaud &
Pouset, France
General Contractor:
ICA, Mexico
Engineering, fabrica-
tion and installation:
Lonas Lorenzo

Architect and project
manager: Roberto
Munoz, Guadalajara,
Mexico
Membrane type:
Polyester substrate
with opaque formulated
vinyl coating
Membrane area:
47,061 m²
Completion: 2010

When the Mexican magnate Jorge Vergara took over Mexico's most famous soccer club Chivas de Guadalajara in 2002,
a new 45,000 seat capacity stadium was
the new president's top priority. The La
Primavera forest was chosen as the ideal
location. The forest with its mountain-
ous surroundings gave birth to the design
of the stadium that was to nestle there.
French architects, Massaud and Pouset,
created a design resembling a volcano
beneath a white cloud (7). The structure
was to be in perfect harmony with its environment, and characterised by the following three elements: volcano slopes
of natural green vegetation to match its
surroundings (3); the inner stand area (2);
a "cloud", that calls to mind a smoking
volcano, designed as a membrane-clad
steel structure (4).

Due to the large spans, lightweight structural solutions were sought. An architectural membrane structure was given preference from an architectural and technical point of view. The main challenge
was to realise the 55,000 m² membrane-
clad underside of "The Cloud": in other
words a ceiling construction in contrast
to the usual roof form. Among the innovative procedures employed was the use of
rope access to facilitate its construction.

A principal requirement was to design "The
Cloud" cover without internal structural
columns (8) and in one piece, originally
spawning the idea of an air-filled, continuous tube. This concept was rejected
for technical and financial reasons.
The chosen stadium roof solution was
planned as a membrane-clad steel truss
structure, resting on 16 giant concrete
columns, towering majestically up to 40 m
over the highest stand.

After developing several models, a design
(5) consisting of 64 wing-like steel pipe
trusses took shape. These were placed
evenly around the pitch with four secondary trusses to connect them. The design
also generated inner and outer compression rings that add more stability and
lightness.

Extensive wind tunnel tests were carried
out in order to develop the most efficient
and robust stadium roof. The goal was to
identify the constant and dynamic wind
load at the site in order to design the stadium structure and its foundations: wind
loads on the façade and the roof (top face
and underside) were required in order to
work out the correct dimensions for the
roof structure and membranes. Based on
the architects' design, a model to a scale

of 1:300 was developed and subjected
to tests that measured wind load, while
taking into account the local geography.
As it was impossible to analyse patterns
for every conceivable wind-load scenario,
focus was placed on the most dominant,
in order to generate the greatest stresses
that the supporting structure would be
subjected to (6).

The initial design incorporated a translucent membrane fabric that was to be illuminated from inside. This choice was later
re-evaluated with regard to the membrane soiling behaviour and the desir-
ability of being able to see the structural
skeleton within. Eventually the decision
was made in favour of an opaque vinyl-
coated fabric (1) that had a special PVDF
finish to encourage a permanently clean,
homogenous look for the membrane.
A textile composite was chosen as the
most durable solution possible and to
provide special surface stability for a roof
that is subjected to considerable stress.
The chosen textile is made using patented
pre-tensioning technology and gained
top marks for its minimal expansion
and alteration when subjected to load.
rp and ws

1 – The membrane structure's underside.

2 – The inner stand area.

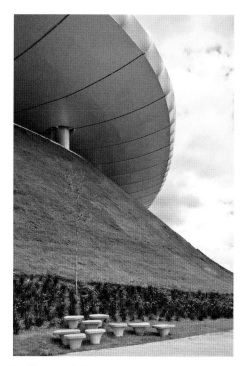

3 – The green "volcano" slopes.

4 – "The Cloud" spectator cover.

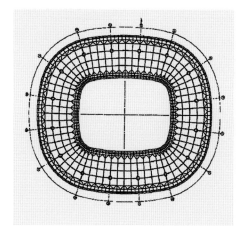

5 – Roof design with 64 segments arranged in 16 blocks with four connecting trusses.

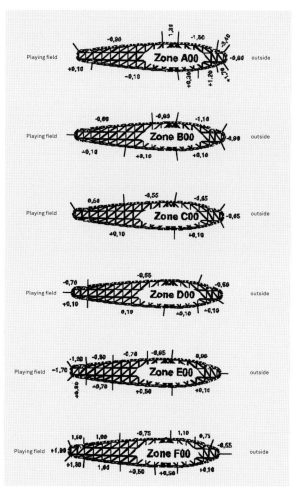

6 – Testing revealed the highest probable wind loads.

7 – Nested in perfect harmony with its surroundings: Omnilife Stadium.

8 – The main requirement: a roof without inner supporting columns.

AP&P CHURCH

Location: Maassluis,
The Netherlands
Building type: Double-
layer insulated mem-
brane structure
Client: AP&P Parochie
Architects: Royal
Haskoning Architecten,
Rotterdam, The Neth-
erlands (Mari Baauw,
René Olivier)
Structural design: Royal
Haskoning, Rotterdam
Membrane design,
analysis and calcula-
tion: Tentech, Utrecht,
The Netherlands

Main contractor:
De Klerk, Werkendam,
The Netherlands
Contractor, membrane:
Buitink Technology,
Duiven, The
Netherlands
Contractor, façade:
Rodeca Systems,
Alphen a/d Rijn,
The Netherlands
Membrane type:
Formulated vinyl-
coated woven polyester,
PVDF varnish
Membrane area:
1,400 m²
Completion: 2007

Upon entering the village of Maassluis, near Rotterdam, the visitor is soon aware of the striking design of the AP&P church. Its futuristic and fluid lines contrast well with the conventional Dutch housing that partially surrounds the building. Maintaining the traditional language of arches, the church was built from several individual shells, overlapping to create the interior. At the shell overlaps, transparent coloured polycarbonate sheeting admits daylight in a manner reminiscent of "stained-glass" (1).

Notwithstanding the contemporary external appearance, the organic shell and "stained-glass" window detail produce a contemplative and peaceful interior (2).

The unconventional form of the roof shells required the evaluation of several construction techniques. The use of profiled steel sheets was initially considered as it provided a relatively inexpensive solution. However its coarse edge detail and irregular interior surface were considerations that prompted a search for alternatives. The idea of covering the profiled sheets with a textile introduced the structural membrane solution. This lightweight technique, which is ideal for semi-permanent coverings, perfectly fitted the architect's concept of a 'material-less' building.

The Maassluis church is an example of a double-layered, insulated membrane structure. The church's shells are supported by tubular steel arches. The steel framework is covered with layers of translucent membrane. Compared to traditional construction systems, this building method requires the membrane stresses to be taken into account. In addition to the self-weight of the structure, the steel arches also carry the loads arising from the tensioning of the membrane. With each double-membrane skin complete with insulation and fixings weighing up to 3500 kg, the membrane must be tensioned to ensure a smooth surface. To avoid deformation of the main steel structure as a result of tensioning and to support the wind and snow loads, a steel substructure interconnects the arches (4).

The double-layered arch structure consists of one membrane layer covering the outer surface of the framework and another covering the inside. The inner and outer membrane sheets are first fastened and tensioned using fabric endpoints secured to steel lugs welded to the tubes. Edge-stiffening cables span between these fixing points to maintain tension in the membranes. To form the shell's weatherproof edge detail, an additional band of textile is wrapped around the tube surface where it broadly overlaps the main inner and outer membrane, to which it is permanently joined by welding (3).

The membrane is a vinyl-coated polyester fabric. The applied membrane has a finishing layer of Teflon. This surface treatment reduces the attraction of airbound particles and, in conjunction with washing by rainwater, keeps the surface clean. To ease construction of the double-curved roof, the 1400 m² surface is divided into 248 separate fabric strips. The strips are welded together to form the finished membrane, which is then fitted with a steel edge-stiffening cable. Intelligent support of the membrane made it possible to tension the structure during installation. Re-tensioning can be carried out during use.

A layer of insulation fits between the outer and the inner skin. This insulation is attached above the inner layer.

The 400–2000 mm cavity space between the two layers is ventilated by openings along the edge of the membrane. In addition to the insulating effect of the double-layered structure, it also responds well to extreme snow and wind loads. Deformations of the outer skin under these loads are accommodated in the cavity space between the two layers. The lightweight shell is thereby able to retain its insulating properties and support the loads, without any resulting deformation being visible from inside the church.

The concept that shaped this church was one of maximum space and light with minimum material. A double-layer insulated membrane provides a contemporary solution for creation of the church's outer shell (5). Daylight enters through the modern transparent polycarbonate windows, which draw upon an ancient "stained-glass" tradition and, in combination with the double-curved ceiling, provide efficient natural lighting. The cohesion of light and space, form and structure, creates an interior that perfectly expresses its function. **rp, ap and iv**

1 – The church's strikingly futuristic shape.

2 – Shell interior.

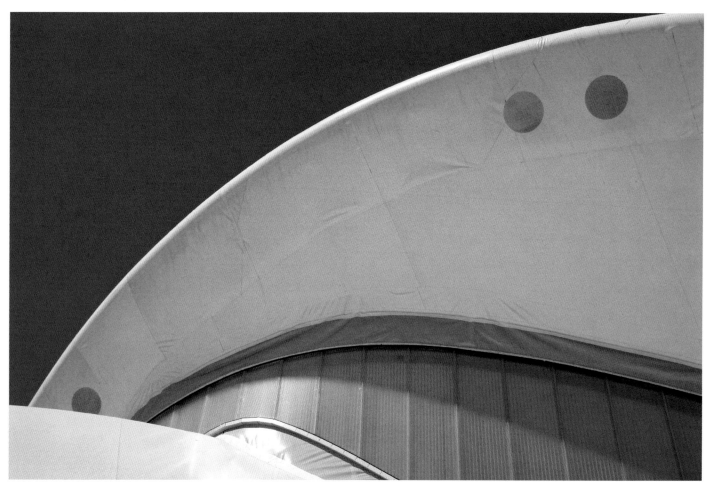

3 – Weatherproof edge detail.

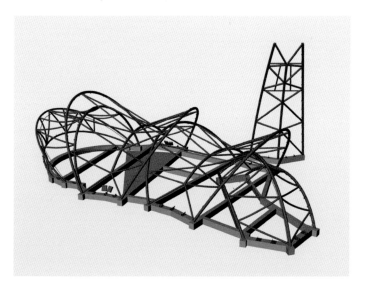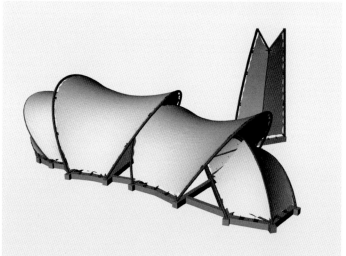

4 – Tubular steel shell frame and principal membrane cover.

5 – Maximising the minimum.

LE LIDO – CIRCUS ARTS CENTER

Location: Toulouse, France
Building type: Cable-supported textile structure
Client: City of Toulouse
Architect: Toulouse City Council, Architecture Management; Pierre-Jean Riera, city council architect
Membrane design and engineering: Prat Structures Avancées, Toulouse

General Contractor: Constructions Saint-Eloi, Toulouse
Contractor for fabrication and installation: VSO France
Membrane: vinyl-coated polyester base cloth with weldable PVDF finish
Membrane area: 2,000 m²
Completion: 2008

Le Lido is a municipal circus school for amateur and professional artists that provides training in the different disciplines while assisting with development of new circus performances. The success of the many renowned trainers and former students has enabled this educational facility to build an outstanding international reputation and today, to train over 500 pupils a year. The design of Le Lido resembles a circus tent or "Big Top", closely reflecting circus culture. This impressive technical textile enclosure covers an area of 1,500 m² (1) and can accommodate 250 spectators while offering a large training area for the students.

The Lido membrane construction is remarkable in that it departs from the traditional circus tent construction using one or more central masts. Instead, a total of eight masts are located in a ring formation around the perimeter of the enclosed area. Each mast is tied to a large central ring element by a network of primary and secondary steel cables. An additional outer network of cables provides the necessary tension to support the ring element and the tensioned textile cover while ensuring overall stability (2). This solution generates high stress within the structure, but results in a large uninterrupted span beneath the membrane. The membrane is made of a high-performance vinyl-coated polyester textile, manufactured using a patented process that pre-tensions the polyester cloth during application of the vinyl coating. This results in a textile with excellent uniformity of coating thickness, which in turn provides high strength, dimensional stability and durability.

In addition to its primary structural role, the central ring element also defines the walls and ceiling of an intimate inner theatre that allows both students and professionals to demonstrate their art to the public. The use of acoustically efficient walls and ceilings for the theatre enclosure provide a 35 dB noise reduction between the stage and the outer membrane shell, thus ensuring the comfort of residents of neighbouring buildings only 100 m away.

As mentioned earlier, the large span is achieved by high tension in the supporting cables. For efficient transfer of the high resultant loads to the eight foundation anchorage points, a newly patented connection system is used (6). This new system allows perfect alignment of the tensioning cables due to the ability of its fastening elements to rotate (5). It also accommodates any additional deformation due to extreme climatic stresses.

Eight large textile panels form the outer membrane of Le Lido. These were initially assembled on the ground and then raised in one piece, allowing assembly in half a day while avoiding unsymmetrical loadings on the steel cable and support structure.

Each of the membrane panels are bordered by an edge stiffening cable (5). Special MagicClamp fastenings at 50 cm centres, link the membrane to its adjacent catenary cable. The fastenings allow fine membrane tension adjustments and hence ensure a smooth wrinkle-free outer surface.

Rain is prevented from penetrating the membrane joints by the provision of aluminium flashings that cover the radial catenary cables (6), and paired aluminium caps and cones (3) that are fastened to stiffening cages to cover the mast heads (4). This solution complements the overall architectural concept. By attention to detail, simplifying cable terminals and avoiding custom-made corner plates the designer has not only generated cost savings, but has achieved a smooth, fluid appearance for this tensioned textile structure.

rp and ws

1 – The distinctive architectural form of Le Lido.

2 – Model showing the principal structural elements: a central ring with
concentric surrounding masts and the supporting cable network.

3 – Le Lido with its characteristic mast caps and cones.

4 – Mast head before covering.

5– Anchoring system detail (membrane edge cable, MagicClamp fastening, external catenary cable, MagicJoint swivel-joint).

6 – The corner anchoring system showing weather proofing and fastening details.

TEXTILE FAÇADES

STÜCKI BUSINESS PARK

Location:
Basel, Switzerland
Building type:
Multi-storey office and
laboratory complex
Client: Swiss Prime
Site AG
Architect: Blaser
Architekten AG, Basel
Engineer, membrane:
Typico GmbH & Co KG,
Lochau, Switzerland

Membrane type:
Polyester/glass-fibre
non-woven base with
polyacrylic coating
finish
Membrane area:
10,500 m^2
Completion:
2011

Dynamic changes are underway in the urban district of North Basel. The site of the former Schetty dye mills, in the meantime converted into Ciba maintenance warehouses, is currently being developed as a prestigious, inspiring and attractive "meeting point" for innovative life-science, IT and nanotechnology companies.

The long building, which has been taking shape since construction started in July 2007, forms the backbone of the Stücki Business Park. The building comprises a base level, with access ramp and elevated road to the first floor entrance level, and six storeys above it. The innovative, 230-metre-long newly developed membrane façade gives the building an unmistakeable identity (1).

The façade is based on a simple but effective concept; a metallic-coloured membrane is tensioned over long asymmetrical triangular prisms formed from welded aluminium frames. Several different asymmetrical prisms are fixed end to end to give an undulating form to the long façades, which serves to break their lines and add movement (3).

In addition, as the prisms overlap the window line they also provide visual interest from inside the building. While asymmetrical, the different prisms are repeated at different locations along the façade, simplifying fabrication of the membrane frames.

Once the membrane façade system had been set up, it was first subjected to full-scale testing (2).

The membrane frames were fabricated from welded aluminium sections. Completed frames were then fastened to the building's concrete façade before fixing the textile membrane covering (4).

In order to stay within the perimeter of the building plot, the south and east façades were manufactured as two-dimensional units, while continuing the same outline shape (3).

The silver-laminated anthracite-coloured membrane fabric was chosen for its transparency, self-cleaning properties, reflective surface and fire resistance. The projected service life of the membrane is 25 years.

The membrane lends the simple rectangular building a strikingly unique appearance on a macro-scale, and gives rise to an interplay of reflections and insights (5). Depending on the viewing angle and the lighting, the building has either a ribbed skeletal look or the appearance of being draped in a light and airy garment, which creates an interplay of light and shadow and lends a sense of lightness to the structure. **rp**

1 – Textile façade.

2 – Testing membrane cladding panels.

3 – West façade nearing completion.

4 – Welded aluminium frames.

5 – Three-dimensional dynamism.

YENDI OFFICE BUILDING

Location:
Bulle, Switzerland
Building type: Multi-storey office building
Client: Yendi S.A.
Architects: deillon delley architectes, Bulle
Contractor: Progin SA Metal, Bulle
Membrane types:
Outer skin: Polyester mesh fabric with formulated vinyl coating, 100% recyclable, permeable.

Inner skin: Breathable, polyacrylate surface coating over non-woven polyester and glass composite membrane
Membrane area: 2,800 m²
Completion: 2007

Yendi, a women's clothing retailer, was founded in 1976, in Bulle, Switzerland. Today, the company has over 80 outlets in Switzerland and has become an international player by expanding its business to neighbouring countries. Yendi's distinctive philosophy of "thinking outside the box" was obvious back in 1999, when it built its logistics centre and took the bold step of wrapping the building in screen-printed textile, an innovative façade solution at the time.

Seven years later, architects Achille Deillon and Alexandre Delley designed another textile façade for Yendi. This façade concept also impressed the management team as the perfect reflection of its business operations (1 and 2).

The concept, destined for the company's new administration building, was to include the textile façade system initially developed by the fabric manufacturer for the logistics building. The façade system consists of an outer skin of vinyl-coated polyester mesh fabric (4),

partnered with a coloured polyacrylic-coated inner façade breather membrane (3) that seals the structure against wind and rain while allowing vapour permeability. The result is a multi-function façade system that greatly contributes to climate control within the building, while giving an impression of depth due to the interplay of light passing through the outer mesh layer and striking the coloured inner membrane.

The new façade design reflects the character of the nearby logistics centre, while at the same time offering a completely new interpretation. To achieve this aim, the architect partnered with the engineering company BCS to produce a mixture of textile façade cladding and sun protection screens, the fabric for which was selected from the same manufacturer to ensure homogeneity of colour. The complementary colour of the inner sealing membrane provides an effect that comes to the fore when the sunscreens move, or when the feeling of depth alters with the changing angle of incidence of the

sun's rays striking the outer façade skin. As a result the façade provides constant movement, thereby adding visual interest (8). Horizontal strips mark the level of the different storeys and accommodate the sunscreens (5), allowing them to disappear so that only the textile façade and metal profiles remain visible (6). The identical façade and sunscreen fabrics create a coherent aesthetic effect, notwithstanding their different functions (7).

Preferences for the textile façade came about as a result of the client's experience with the logistics building. Furthermore, the choice was strongly influenced by the technical textile's durability, robustness and resistance to tearing. The façade system provides a high level of solar protection, ventilation and insulation, thereby ensuring excellent climate control within the building, a function that was further enhanced by this new design.

rp and ws

1 – General exterior view.

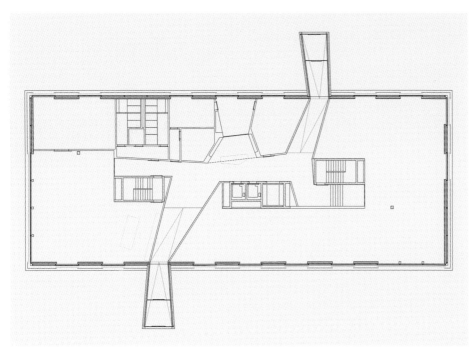

2 – Reception-level floor plan.

3 – Breathable inner membrane behind outer mesh fabric.

4 – Detail of outer mesh fabric.

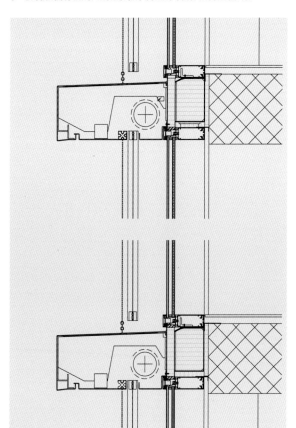

5 – Section: horizontal "strips" house the sunscreen mechanism.

6 – Sunscreens raised, façade membrane and metal profiles visible.

7 – Coherent façade elements.

8 – Changing sunscreen positions ...

... add visual interest.

DEICHMANN FLAGSHIP STORE

Location:
Essen, Germany
Building type: Multi-
storey flagship store
Client: Heinrich
Deichmann-Schuhe
GmbH & Co. KG
Architects: Planungs-
gruppe Drahtler GmbH,
Dortmund, Germany
Membrane engineer:
Tensoforma Trading srl,
Entratico, Italy

Contractor: Zompras
Metallbau GmbH,
Soest, Germany
Membrane type:
Polyester mesh fabric
with formulated vinyl
coating.
100% recyclable.
Membrane area: 550 m²
Completion: 2008

Deichmann's new flagship store on Lim-becker Platz in Essen city centre is a new and striking enhancement to the area. After demolishing the existing building, used by the client since 1994, a new five-storey Deichmann flagship store with floor space of 2,000 m² was constructed.

As a contrast to the huge, dominant build-ing opposite (a shopping centre with a perforated plate façade) greater unity was sought for the new facade (1). At the same time, it was to have a high level of transparency in order to ensure the flagship store had a close link to the out-side world. The objective was very clear: to showcase the inside from the outside. At the same time, the client also wanted a high level of transparency to the outside so that customers could enjoy the view.

After considering various approaches, the textile façade concept was the most con-vincing. In addition to the high level of transparency and performance, it was above all the availability of the chosen textile in 27 colours that swung the de-cision, the "hammered metal" tone being selected. This tone was a very good match for the mix of construction materials and in addition, blended well with the metal-lic look of the building opposite.

Another benefit of the textile façade was that curved panels were possible (2); op-timal use of the site's land registry bor-ders led to design of the building envelope such that it would "flow" into the avail-able area.

The basis of the façade is a post/beam design in a dark grey mica-like tone with glass elements, some of which can be opened. The ground floor includes a poly-gonal shop window comprising curved glass elements. At approximately 550 m² the textile membrane covers the largest area of the façade (3) and has the Deich-mann lettering and logo digitally printed onto the textile (4). The Italian textile façade system comprises 1.25 x 3.60 m format aluminium frame units, over which the textile membrane is tensioned. Fab-rication details for the curved and flat façade units were similar as are the fast-ening details. The membrane surfaces are interrupted at floor level by ceramic panels (5), which also cover the transi-tion walls to the neighbouring buildings.

The designer's challenge was to develop a corporate architectural concept that would serve the client as a model for stores at other sites. The brand image was to be projected externally without additional illuminated elements or logos that would detract from the harmonious aesthetic of the façade. The choice of a textile façade enabled the architect to satisfy the client's requirements with a high-quality and cost-effective solution.

rp and ws

1 – Style and transparency at Limbecker Platz, Essen, Germany.

2 – Curved façade for optimum use of floor space.

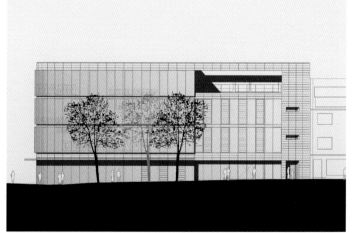

3 – Elevations showing the relative areas of textile membrane,
glazed surface and ceramic tiles.

4 – Lettering digitally printed onto the textile.

5 – Rectangular ceramic panels define storey levels.

6 – Fixing detail: adjacent flat panels to vertical mullion.

GERMAN PAVILION "BALANCITY" AT EXPO 2010 SHANGHAI

Location: Shanghai, China
Building type:
EXPO Pavilion
Client: Federal Ministry
of Economics and
Technology
Organisation/Operation:
Koelnmesse International
GmbH, Cologne, Germany
Architects/general plan-
ning: Schmidhuber + Kaindl
GmbH, Munich, Germany
Concept, fabrication and
installation:
TAIYO KOGYO China

Media and exhibition
design: Milla und Partner
GmbH, Stuttgart, Germany
General contractor: Nüssli
Deutschland GmbH, Roth,
Germany
Membrane type:
Polyester mesh fabric with
formulated vinyl coating,
100% recyclable
Membrane area: 12,000 m²
Completion: 2010

The "balancity" design (1) by Munich architects Schmidhuber + Kaindl is the German response to the EXPO 2010 "Better City, Better Life" theme; a city that balances innovation with tradition, urban aspects with nature, and globalisation with national identity. The pavilion (2) illustrates the EXPO's core theme at a glance; an opposing collection of elements, which unite in equilibrium.

For the architectural design of the pavilion, Schmidhuber + Kaindl opted for a powerful, sculptural character (4). This aspect was to be enhanced by transparency; rooms flooded with light, a sense of weightlessness and flexibility. A textile façade fabric was chosen as the material to underscore this aspect in the most sustainable manner. The fabric flexibly covers the building like a second skin.

Constant change was a key theme of the design. Change is emphasised by the silver textile façade fabric that reflects the ambient light. For example, the building is captured by a reddish light at sunrise, resembles a silver crystal in bright daylight (9), or is highlighted by the stark night-time contrast between the silvery, textile building shell and the reflected light from the grassed area beneath it (8).

Another core theme of the pavilion's design was the blurring of borders between inside and outside. A particular example is the wall of the VIP lounge that develops from the outside façade, segues into the tunnel and becomes the stair's handrail before eventually losing itself again within the huge body of the structure (3).

The additional design dimension created by the fabric's transparency becomes apparent when walking inside the building. While much of the fabric is opaque, areas of transparent textile reveal striking views of the outside (6). Depending on their location, people perceive a succession of different angles and impressions.

Another important factor in favour of the textile façade was the recycling option at the end of EXPO 2010. Preparatory work for this was completed at the beginning of 2011. Under supervision of the general contractor Nüssli, the full structure was taken down (7). Some of the fabric could be re-used at the German School in Shanghai while approximately 11,000 m² remain for recycling. This will entail the removal of non-textile parts such as metal ropes, eyelets and tubing. The recovered fabric can then be tightly packed onto pallets for transportation by container to the manufacturer's Texyloop plant in Ferrara. Here fabrics are fully recycled, with 70% used as PVC granulate and 30% as polyester fibres, raw material for many new products.
rp and ws

1 – The "balancity" pavilion.

2 – An elegant equilibrium of opposing elements.

3 – The outside membrane becomes the inside.

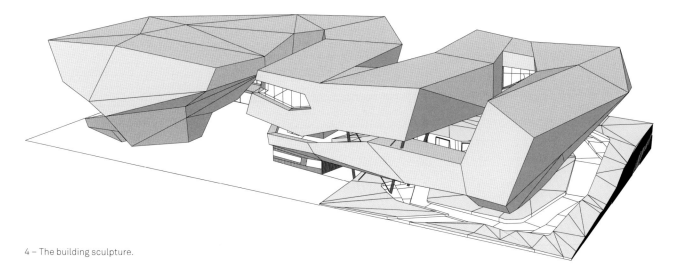

4 – The building sculpture.

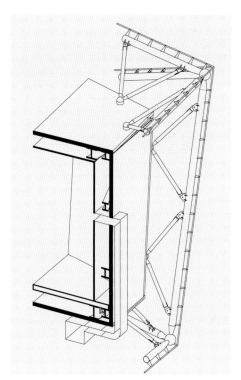

6 – Striking view revealed.

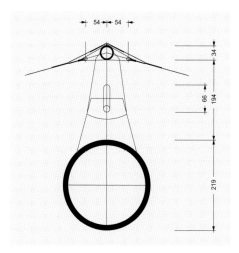

5 – Membrane panel fixing details.

7 – Recovering the membrane for recycling.

8 – Stark textural contrasts abound.

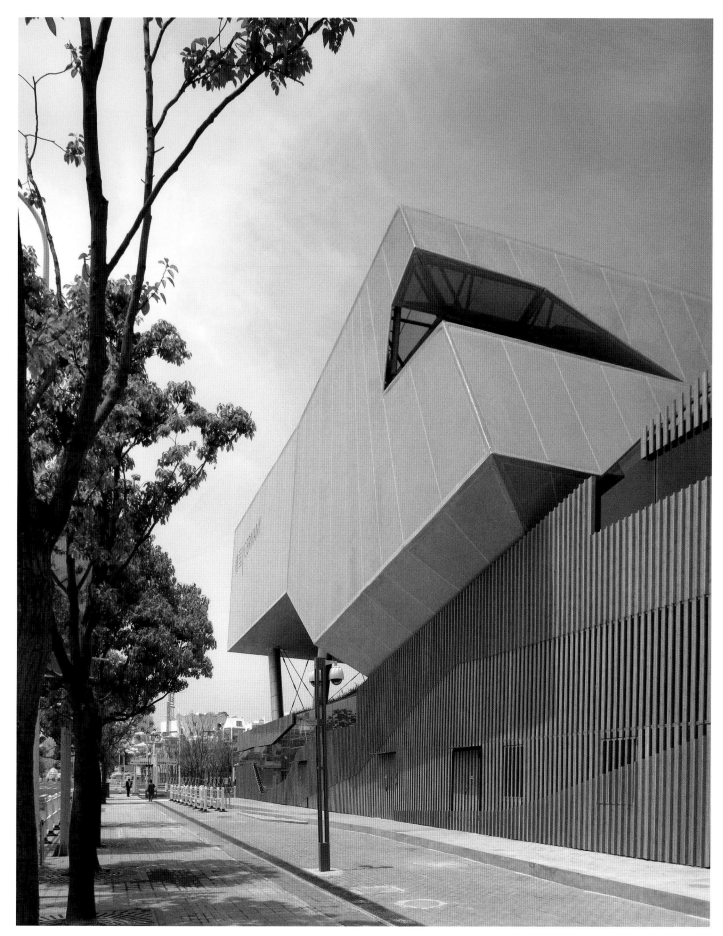

9 – The building resembles a silver crystal in daylight.

KERAMIKLAND SHOWROOM AND OFFICE BUILDING

Location:
Cham, Switzerland
Building type:
three-storey building
Client: Keramikland AG
Architect: Hans Schwegler, architect HTL/STV, Ufhusen, Switzerland
Façade construction and installation: HP Gasser AG, Lungern, Switzerland
Membrane manufacturing: Mehotex, Burgdorf, Switzerland

Membrane type:
Outer skin: high-tenacity glass fibre mesh coated with PTFE
Inner skin: breathable, polyacrylate surface coating over non-woven polyester and glass composite membrane
Membrane area: 1,073 m²
Completion: 2011

Keramikland is a retailer and interior design company for first-class bathrooms and sanitary products. For the company's new showroom centre in central Switzerland, a former service point belonging to a heating company was to be converted and adapted to requirements.

The chosen site was a disparate collection of buildings, comprising a reception, customer service area, workshop, offices and a warehouse. The architect was confronted by buildings of varying floor levels and heights. In addition to this challenge, there was also the problem of integrating the different windows; the warehouse had none, while the workshops were large and the office windows narrow.

The client's key requirement was for an innovative façade with a prestigious look to reflect the company's standards and the high quality of its products. The basis of the building concept was to add height to the office and service area in order to obtain a unifying cuboid structure. To achieve a smooth appearance, architect Hans Schwegler used a double-skin membrane solution, of which the transparent outer skin partially screens the windows. A monolithic structure with sophisticated black textile cladding was thus created, its principal façade only interrupted by the contrasting white of the company name and the eye-catching entrance area (1).

An advantage of the textile used for the outer façade skin is its ability to allow the required level of natural lighting via the existing windows. Its transparency ensures a high level of visual comfort for people working in the offices (3) and provides good natural illumination of the showroom displays. The textile façade acts as a screen to block out sun and glare in summer, while ample light enters the building even when the sky is obscured by clouds. The fabric's transparency provides an additional attractive effect when the building's interior is artificially lit. During the day the building has a monolithic character, but at night the transparency of the textile allows the different-sized windows to appear, thereby adding visual interest.

The outer skin – the textile façade cladding – comprises a fibre glass composite membrane with PTFE surface, the inner skin – the weather protection sealing – a breathable polyester/glass non-woven membrane with polyacrylate coating. The double-skin façade solution reduces the energy required for climate control within the building; solar heated air rises in the ventilation space between the inner and outer skins, thereby avoiding excessive heating of the façade. Hence the breathable façade inner membrane contributes to a solution that provides optimum protection from the environment. In addition, the façade complies with strict local fire-protection regulations.

Black galvanised consoles were fastened onto the sub-structure, which was clad with the inner breathable membrane to support the anodised aluminium profiles that provide the mounting for the outer skin (4). The components of the outer skin fastenings (c) were customised for the project by the installation specialist. The stainless steel rope (b) anchors the fabric (a) into the Keder rail (d), and final textile post-tensioning adjustments can be made using the stainless steel bolts (e).

The double-skin membrane solution allowed the architect to achieve his client's objectives with a façade enclosure that successfully unifies the former building elements, producing an eye-catching renovation that breaths new life into this industrial site (2). **rp and ws**

1 – The textile façade with contrasting white signage and entrance areas.

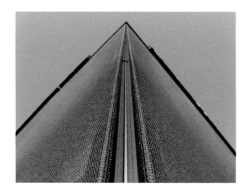

2 – An eye-catching architectural textile façade solution.

3 – High visual comfort for the office staff.

4 – Aluminium profile system for outer-skin fixing and tensioning.
a: PTFE-coated fibre-glass fabric
b: Stainless steel rope in fabric pocket
c: Stainless steel tensioning bolt
d: Aluminium Keder-rail extrusion
e: Aluminium frame extrusion

SEDE iGUZZINI ILLUMINAZIONE ESPAÑA

Location:
Barcelona, Spain
Building type:
Four-storey office
building
Client: iGuzzini Illumi-
nazione España
Architects: MiAS
Architects, Barcelona
Engineering/fabrication
and installation:
Iaso, Lleida, Spain

Membrane type:
Polyester mesh with
formulated vinyl
coating
Membrane area:
1,600 m²
Completion:
2010

Located at one of Barcelona's major traffic hubs, development of the new Spanish headquarters for the lighting manufacturer iGuzzini proved quite a challenge. The architectural firm MiAS contrasted the busy industrial reality of the project site with an eye-catching ellipsoidal structure that engages the imagination. The resultant building rises from a concrete podium, the activity within shrouded by an outer composite membrane (8).

The design comprises a central vase-shaped tubular steel structure, which entirely supports four floors of workspace arranged as a stack of rings. A second skin of high-performance composite material wraps around the southern façade, providing climate control for the building's interior as well as defining its shape. The central steel support structure also serves as a light shaft for the building's interior workspaces, creating a fascinating juxtaposition of natural and artificial light.

Energy saving and sustainability form an integral part of the building's design, a requirement made more demanding by the inclusion of room-height glazed façades at all floor levels. In this respect the decision to add a transparent outer skin not only creates a striking appearance but allows an overall improvement in the building's energy efficiency, a solution largely dependent on the performance characteristics of the chosen technical textile. The composite material is manufactured from an open-weave polyester fabric. A formulated vinyl coating has been applied to both sides of the fabric by the Précontraint process, thus ensuring uniformity of coating thickness. The resultant composite material is dimensionally stable, self-cleaning, and has a service life of the order 25 to 30 years. Its open structure provides ample transparency for the required internal daylight levels, while protecting the inner glazed façade from solar radiation (1). This, together with protection from wind and rain, creats a buffer zone between the building envelope and the outside environment. The membrane solution thus provides a means of reducing the energy required for climate control and, together with the central light shaft, for artificial lighting; two important factors that ensure the comfort of the building's occupants.

The composite membrane is continuous around the southern façade, opening at the north face to reveal the building's inner skin (2). A key feature of this project is the precision of membrane fabrication and installation. This is made possible by the dimensional stability of the textile. The membrane and its sub-structure were developed using computer-aided design and 3-D modelling to define both the textile panel cutting pattern and the node position for membrane fastening. The components were thus manufactured and assembled to great accuracy, using high-frequency electromagnetic welding to ensure membrane quality (9). The membrane fasteners comprise bolted twin metal discs that sandwich and firmly grip the textile (5). They, in turn, are fixed to multi-function metal anchorage nodes that connect square section steel tubes arranged in a triangular form, somewhat reminiscent of a geodesic dome (6). The resultant lattice forms the membrane's supporting sub-structure. The central screw fixing of the membrane fastener assembly allows textile tension adjustment after initial fixing (7 and 10). The multi-function anchorage nodes are themselves bolted to vertical tubular steel frames, of which there are ten uniformly spaced around the building's inner façade (3). The composite membrane captures the geometry of the triangular elements and lends the façade a particularly dynamic look, thanks to a diagonal striped design of alternate silver and grey tones, selected from a broad palette of available colours.

The façade solution with composite material thus allowed creation of the building's eye-catching shape, while enhancing the efficiency of its internal lighting and climate control. The building users benefit from a high level of comfort, a clear view of the surroundings, and an attractive structure (4). **rp and ws**

1 – A membrane for substantial reduction of light and heat transmission.

2 – The north face membrane opens to reveal the glass façade.

3 – Tubular steel frames support the membrane sub-structure.

4 – Visual comfort combined with glare protection.

5 – Ring-shaped membrane fasteners.

6 – The triangular lattice sub-structure awaiting membrane placement.

7 – Initial placement and fastening of the membrane.

8 – Textile architecture as modern sculpture.

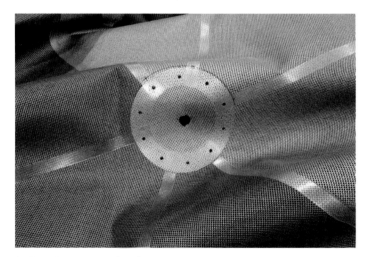

9 – Precision cutting and welding are essential elements of the membrane manufacture.

10 – The membrane after tensioning.

SOLAR
PROTECTION

RIFFA VIEWS INTERNATIONAL SCHOOL

Location:
Manama, Bahrain
Building type: Swim-
ming pool shade and
façade solar protection
Client: Riffa Views
International School
Architect/engineers:
Mohamed Salahuddin
Consulting Engineer-
ing Bureau, Architects
and Engineers, MSCEB,
Manama

Contractor, fabricator
and installer:
Gulf Shade, Manama
Membrane type:
Open-weave polyester
fibre with formulated
vinyl coating and acrylic
lacquer finish
Membrane area:
2,300 m²
Completion: 2009

A technical textile solution provides solar protection over the pool area of the Riffa Views International School in Bahrain, satisfying the principal design objective of maintaining the notion of an open sky while protecting swimmers from the intense sunlight (2). In addition the membrane concept is applied as solar protection to the building façade (1).

A textile membrane canopy was perfectly adapted to the geometry of the site. The 45 by 35 metre pool area is bordered on two sides by the school building; a reinforced concrete wall screens the remaining two sides of the pool. The school building provides anchorage for the canopy along one edge. The opposing edge is anchored by corner plates to steel masts. The masts are arranged as a reticulated "A" frame, fixed to and using the concrete wall as support. This steel structure comprises eight membrane fixing points at the top of columns, the final fixing being located on the main building (3). The façade membrane panels are fastened between similar "A" frame steel structures, for architectural design continuity (1).

The chosen fabric was made from an open-weave coated polyester fibre, with a fabric weight of 820 g/m². The material was chosen for its high resistance to solar radiation and its recyclability. The projected lifetime of the fabric is greater than ten years. Before patterning, bi-axial testing was conducted to estimate the required compensation for this type of fabric, an important factor needed to determine fabric elongation during the pre-stressing stage.

The fabric cutting pattern was carefully planned as this would not only affect the visual aspect of the finished structure but would avoid waste when cutting the fabric strips. In this particular case the best option was for the individual membrane strips to be oriented perpendicular to the length of the canopy.

The membrane design was generated in 3D space by the utilization of specific tensile structure software (4). The generated form was selected in terms of elegance, shape, and curvature.

The load on the membrane was calculated assuming a typical wind speed of 40m/s and the structural analysis carried out accordingly. Various wind load scenarios were modelled to verify the stability of the structure. The result of the structural analysis was then used to design and size the membrane cables and fittings, and the supporting steel masts and struts. A range of membrane corner plates was fabricated to suit each type of fastening location (5). **rp**

1 – Façade solar protection canopies.

2 – Pool protection canopy.

3 – Canopy and composite supporting structure.

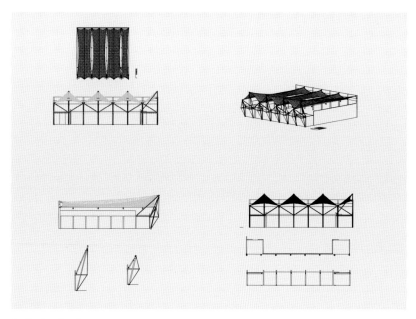

4 – Design drawings.

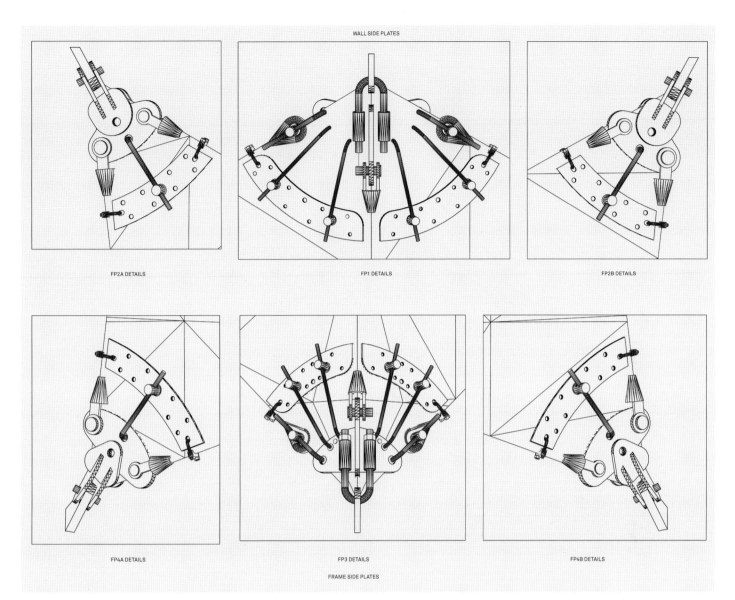

FP2A DETAILS

FP1 DETAILS

FP2B DETAILS

FP4A DETAILS

FP3 DETAILS

FP4B DETAILS

FRAME SIDE PLATES

5 – Corner plate details.

6 – General view of the textile canopy's integration with the school complex.

SHADE – SHADOW COURTYARD

Location: Riyadh, Saudi Arabia

Client: Saad Ben Laden

Architect/engineer: Ali Smaili, King Saud University, Riyadh

Engineers, membrane: Société Libanaise des Industries Réunies

(SLIR), Lebanon and Saudi Arabia

Membrane type: Polyester fibre fabric with PVDF coating

Membrane area: 125 m²

Completion: 2009

Given the historical importance of nomadic tent structures in the desert, contemporary membrane structures find a ready cultural niche in Saudi Arabia. This case history looks at a modern solution to the need for solar protection as applied to the courtyard of a home in Riyadh. The climate in Saudi Arabia, intense sunlight with high temperatures, presents considerable design challenges. The sun's rays can damage not only human skin but also the membrane textile.

In terms of the architectural solution the shape is simple. For the principal shaded area, three horizontal sails are interlinked; each membrane surface forms a shallow hyperbolic parabola (1 and 2). The sails are disposed horizontally and partially overlapped. As the sun crosses the sky the shade pattern changes, becoming most protective during the hottest period of the day. The sails are oriented to collect and channel air currents to the shaded area beneath them. So while the shape is simple the deployment of the membrane canopy provides an elegant and efficient solar shade. At the far end of the courtyard a further similar membrane canopy is used to shade an entrance to the house.

The textile chosen for the sails (5) was selected for its ability to withstand extreme atmospheric conditions. The textile's polyester fibres are formed by the patented Précontraint process which provides exceptional resistance to UV exposure. The textile has a highly concentrated PVDF (polyvinylidene fluoride) surface treatment that ensures long-term cleanability, thereby reducing maintenance cost to the owner. Furthermore it is 100% recyclable, an important consideration given the ever-present need to conserve the natural environment.

Structurally, the design criteria took account of the following loads: the membrane pre-stress, the wind pressure, and the sand load. The membrane corner plates, edge stiffening cables and their fixings are all made of stainless steel (4).

The wall anchorages (3) comprise base plates made from galvanised steel. After bolting to the masonry walls the plate fixings are hidden behind a decorative steel cover. The choice of metals for anchorage fabrication was made weighing cost and durability against aesthetics. The climate in Riyadh is very dry and hence the corrosion risk for this application is low. The anchorages were fixed using standard tools and access materials, after which the membrane installation and tensioning operation was swiftly undertaken by the specialist installer. **rp**

1 – Shade and shadow.

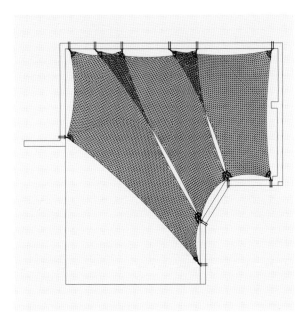

2 – Plan view of the canopies.

3 – Connection to the structure of the house.

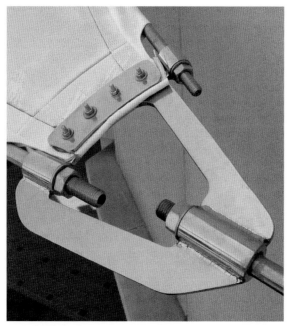

4 – Membrane corner plate and anchorage detail.

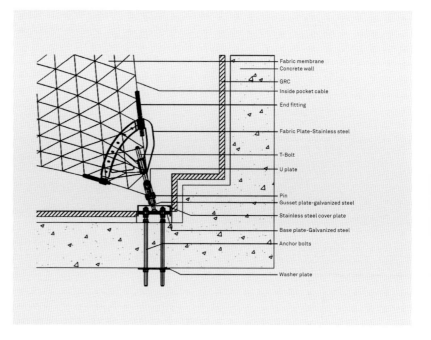

Fabric membrane
Concrete wall
GRC
Inside pocket cable
End fitting
Fabric Plate-Stainless steel
T-Bolt
U plate
Pin
Gusset plate-galvanized steel
Stainless steel cover plate
Base plate-Galvanized steel
Anchor bolts
Washer plate

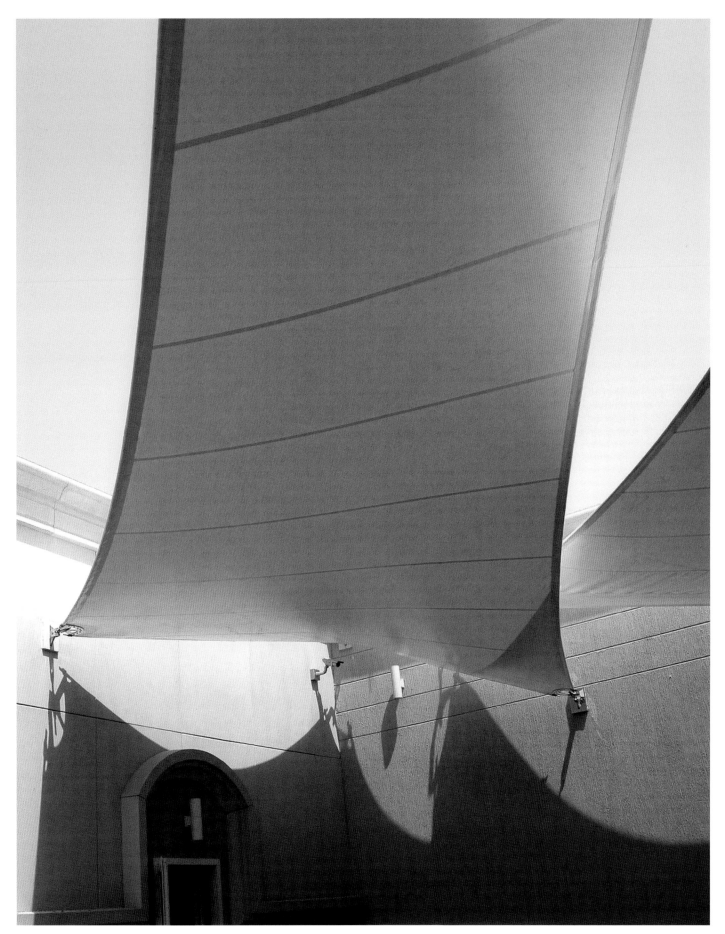

5 – Textile subjected to aggressive UV exposure.

OFFICE BUILDING

Location:
Basel, Switzerland
Building type: Five-
storey office building
Client: Novartis
Pharma AG
Architects: Gehry
Partners, LLP,
Los Angeles, USA
General management/
project management:
ANW Arcoplan / Nissen
& Wentzlaff General-
planer, Basel
Climate concept: Trans-
solar, Munich, Germany

Engineering, manufac-
ture and installation
of the solar protection
equipment:
clauss markisen
Projekt GmbH,
Bissingen-Ochsen-
wang, Germany
Membrane type:
Polyester mesh sub-
strate with vinyl coating
and Low-E treatment
Membrane area:
10,000 m²
Completion:
2010

The office building with auditorium, developed by Gehry Partners, LLP, is distinctive for the architect's typical deconstructivist way of playing with shapes. It stands apart with its free-style shapes that flow into one another and its opulent transparency and openness. (1) It is formed as a glass sculpture representing multiple box-like structures with interlocking façades. Design of the solar protection system was very challenging due to the irregular angles and curvatures of the façades; this in turn required high performance from the technical textile used in its construction. In addition to large formats and complex shapes, a range of technical specifications such as Low-E (Low Emissivity) had to be fulfilled.

Solar protection for the complex, multi-façade building shell was provided by internally mounted large textile panels fabricated in three basic shapes: triangle, rectangle and trapezoid. The textile panels unroll from opposed tubular supports and are shaped so that when fully extended a continuous solar screen is formed (2 to 4). Coverage of the varying façade surfaces was achieved by changing alignments of the textile panel's tubular supports, of which there are 412 in total (5).

Sustainable development was the watchword during design; the building's climate control is managed by a sophisticated interaction of elements. The external facade uses triple glazing with appropriate Low-E coating together with integrated ventilation. The internal solar protection system provides a high level of screening while remaining transparent, and also benefits from a Low-E coating. Even the roof surfaces play a role, incorporating solar panels for electrical power production and increased solar shading, as well as water-cooled white lamella, which serve to diffuse sunlight while reducing thermal loading.

The solar protection textile was required to guarantee 57% light reflection and 22 % transmission and has a Low-E coating of 0.48 maximum emissivity. The solar energy striking the building's solar protection system is partly reflected by the screening fabric, and partially absorbed by the material. The build-up of heat that results is dispersed over a large area by two mechanisms: convection of the heated air and by radiation. Hence, while the solar panels are heated due to the inclination of the façade areas, the Low-E rating suppresses this radiation. The triple glazing and solar protection systems work together to provide a façade of high thermal efficiency. This has a significant effect on the feeling of comfort experienced within the building.

In addition to the appropriate fire protection characteristics, high performance was required of the technical textile selected for fabrication of the solar screens. This structure provides a further illustration of the diversity of technical textile solutions. In harmony with the building's architecture, this solar protection solution provides a very comfortable and efficient working environment.

rp and ws

1 – Striking deconstructivist architecture: the office building in Basel designed by Gehry Partners, LLP.

2 – Interlocking retractable textile screens provide high-level solar protection.

3 – In addition to radiating little heat, the material used is transparent and dimensionally stable.

4 – The internal solar screens integrate seamlessly with the architecture while ensuring a generously lit workspace.

5 – Screens at point of interlock showing installation detail.

THE DOLDER GRAND HOTEL

Location:
Zurich, Switzerland
Building type: Spa Hotel
General Contractor:
Dolder Hotel AG
Architects:
Foster + Partners,
Riverside Three, London, Great Britain
General management/
project management:
Itten + Brechbühl AG,
Zurich

Solar protection engineering/installation:
Kästli & Co. AG, Bern,
Switzerland
Membrane type: Two
different weave densities of polyester mesh
substrate with formulated vinyl coating
Membrane area:
approx. 2,000 m²
Completion:
2008

With the refurbishment of the famous hotel "The Dolder Grand" in Zurich, Sir Norman Foster confidently creates a bridge between tradition and modernism. The principal design objective was to carefully accentuate the original building as the central feature. Foster + Partner's typical style is above all reflected in the extensions grouped around the main building:
– an egg-shaped ballroom built into the adjacent hillside;
– a garden level with restaurant and a large conference area;
– two extensions that frame the original building, the golf and the spa wing (1).

The hotel occupies a prominent position on the south-facing slope of Adlisberg, a hill overlooking Zurich. This, together with numerous regulations on the protection of historical buildings, placed very exacting requirements on the design of the hotel's solar protection screens.

The first challenge was the wide variety of screens required: ranging from retractable dome awnings, traditional and classic awnings (5 and 6), to retractable vertical and inclined screens (3). Due to the nature of the project and the desire to achieve a homogeneous appearance, a high-quality textile was sought. The chosen vinyl-coated polyester mesh fabric was specified with two different mesh weaves for variation of transparency according to

the screen location; the designer wished to take every advantage afforded by the hotel's spectacular views. The textile is made by the patented Précontraint manufacturing process, which not only ensures that the fabric's vinyl coating is uniform but also results in a strong yet thin material. This enabled the solar screen shutter boxes to be compact and unobtrusive.

A particular characteristic of the façade design is the "Dolder nose". It reflects the slightly projecting, distinctive edge to the roof, while integrating the solar screens that shade the south-facing patios. The screen's textile panel is fastened into a moulded channel in the anodised aluminium beam that forms the screen's rigid leading edge when opened. When closed, the beam's surface closely integrates with the underside of the "Dolder" nose. During the detailed design, care was taken to find the right compromise between maximum shading and spacing between each of the awnings while maintaining the wave shape of the façade (4).

Large vertical screens, 2 x 5 m in size, are provided to screen the conference area (2). Due to the exposed position, these have to support wind speeds of up to 60 km/h. Here the chosen fabric proved to be entirely suitable because of its high tearing resistance and dimensional stability, properties enhanced by

the Précontraint process. It also offered excellent screening and glare protection, combined with a high level of transparency. Additional stiffeners were added to each vertical screen in the form of horizontal glass-fibre rods, sewn into the textile. This solution, borrowed from boat sail manufacture, ensures that the screens can support the pressures arising from the high wind loads. The chosen textile was also suitable for covering the table parasols, thus ensuring a homogeneous appearance.

The balconies of the hotel's new spa and golf extensions are also equipped with retractable awnings of similar design to those previously mentioned (7). The screen's leading-edge supporting beam has a cross-section that enables it to integrate unobtrusively into the architectural detailing of the façade. The design provides the necessary screen stiffness to resist the region's high wind speeds, and to allow the screen widths to be varied in order to follow the façade's concave and convex curves.

The high performance of the chosen technical textile enabled a flexible solution to the challenging task of realising the high-quality solar protection screens required for this refurbishment project. **rp and ws**

1 – Modernism meets tradition: the golf wing extension in front of the original building.

2 – A demanding challenge for large-format solar protection screens.

3 – Fixed inclined awnings over a patio.

4 – Precision engineering allows the solar screens to follow the façade curvature.

5 – A panoply of solar screens.

6 – Retractable vertical and inclined awnings of the extension wing.

7 – The retractable inclined awnings seen here in another perspective.

8 – Vertical terrace awnings.

PAUL KLEE CENTER

Location:
Bern, Switzerland
Building type:
Museum building
Client: Maurice E.
and Martha Müller
Foundation
Architects: Renzo Piano
Building Workshop,
Paris, and ARB Arbeits-
gruppe, Bern
Structural engineering
and planning:
Ove Arup & Partners,
B+S Ingenieure

Solar protection manu-
facturing/installation:
Storama, Burgistein,
Switzerland
Membrane:
Polyester mesh sub-
strates with formulated
vinyl coating
Membrane area:
2,700 m²
Completion: 2006

The art collection of the Paul Klee Centre and its 4,000 works is the world's biggest of its kind, comprising paintings, water-colours and drawings from all of the artist's creative periods. In addition to show-casing the works, the Centre's key role is to provide academic analysis of Paul Klee's artistic, pedagogical and theoretical work and present it to visitors in a comprehensible form.

In planning the new Paul Klee Centre, the famous architect Renzo Piano was convinced from the very beginning that this artist had too much depth to be locked into an "ordinary" building. Piano called the artist the "poet of silence" and wanted to create a museum that suggested a feeling of serenity.

Looking at the site for the first time, Renzo Piano was inspired by the surrounding area. He identified the undulating hills and the motorway – a timeline of civilisation – as the special characteristics of the location that lent it its identity. Based on the rules governing the composition of traditional paintings Piano sketched three hills, as an expression of the surrounding terrain, and the new structure became a landscape sculpture. The middle "hill" is dedicated to the Bernese artist's painting collection. A multi-purpose, concert and event hall, as well as children's museum, is located in the north "hill", while the south hill accommodates a research centre (1).

Although the spectacular roof line is clearly discernible from the motorway for about 10 seconds, viewed from the park, it is not immediately clear whether the three mysterious undulating forms are artificial or natural. However, when standing in front of the main façade, its impressive dimensions reveal themselves: the "hills" are up to 19 m high at the ridge (6) with a glass façade that extends 150 m along the line of the motorway.

As the majority of works displayed in the Paul Klee Centre are sensitive to light and cannot be subjected to more than 80 lux, precise control of light falling on the paintings by solar screening is of paramount importance. The following comparisons illustrate the significance of this constraint to the designer. On a sunny July day about 100,000 lux would enter without additional protection, while during a cloudy March day the light intensity would still be of the order 10,000 lux. Nonetheless, and notwithstanding the essential requirement to control light entering the building, the designer still wished to create a special atmosphere of illumination and transparency.

In order to prevent the sun's rays from entering directly, the museum is lit from the western façade (3). This has large motor-driven exposed awnings, specially developed for the project (2). Solar protection is completed by additional vertical textile screens, secured by cables tensioned between cast-aluminium consoles (7). The consoles, indicative of the overall attention to detail, were designed by the architect and implemented by the solar protection installation company. A further challenge lay in the sheer size of the vertical screens, extending up to 9 m high. Because of the façade's exposed position, wind tunnel tests were carried out. The solar protection system was thus proven for wind speeds of up to 180 km/h, well in excess of the worst-case scenario.

The search for a suitable fabric was concluded when the solar protection manufacturer introduced a vinyl-coated poly-ester textile with the required performance characteristics. The fabric reduces light transmission to the levels required while remaining sufficiently transparent to ensure the building's occupants a clear view of the outside. Manufactured using the Précontraint technology, the fabric has excellent dimensional stability, making it suitable for large-format applications (4). In addition, the material has a low unit weight and a thin section, thereby allowing the solar screen's fixtures and fittings to be slender and unobtrusive (5). These characteristics, plus an availability in a wide range of colours, matched the architect's requirements perfectly. **rp, ws and jv**

1 – Landscape sculpture by Renzo Piano.

2 – Detail of motor-driven retractable awnings.

3 – Complex solar protection comprising vertical screens and retractable sail-like awnings.

4 – Large formats and asymmetrical screen design require good dimensional stability.

5 – The exceptionally thin lightweight textile allows the use of compact fixtures.

6 – The impressive 19 m high façade.

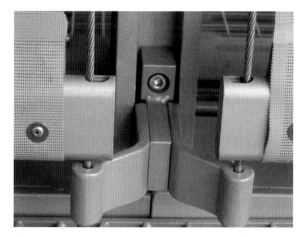

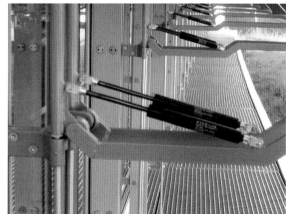

7 – Sunscreen cable runners tensioned at custom-made consoles.

INTERIOR
TEXTILES

CHANTEREYNE POOL

Location: Cherbourg-Octeville, France
Building type: Covered swimming pool
Client: Town of Cherbourg-Octeville
Architects: Thierry Nabères Architectes (TNA), Paris, with Bésuelle et Salley, Cherbourg-Octeville

Contractor for fabrication and installation: ACS production, Montoir de Bretagne, France
Membrane type: Open-weave polyester fibre with formulated vinyl coating and acrylic lacquer finish.
Membrane area: 1,400 m²
Completion: 2007

Occupying an important position in the city, between the port and city centre, the Chantereyne pool and sports complex is typical of 1960s architecture. The renovation of the original reinforced concrete building was initiated in 2004. The project offers a contemporary enhancement, while reproducing the proportions of the original building. This case study looks at the use of interior textiles for the internal ceiling surface (1).

The reinforced concrete frame of the original building (2) was found to be in good condition and was therefore retained and completely renovated.

The choice of a technical textile for the internal ceiling harmonises with the clean modern textures selected for other surfaces of the building. The chosen textile is a vinyl-coated open-weave polyester fabric with an acrylic lacquer finish. Its properties, dimensional stability in a humid and high-chloride environment,

together with an open structure allowing air circulation, make it ideal for this application given the potentially corrosive environment typically found within indoor pool buildings.

The alternating bi-planar disposition of the ceiling's membrane sheets, coupled with the materials inherent sound-absorbing qualities, contribute significantly to reducing echo within the pool hall.

The renovation of this reinforced concrete structure has succeeded in transforming a structure that was very much a product of the 1960s into a modern, vibrant and welcoming local water sports centre (3). The policy of renewable development has been applied at every level, not least in the choice of a technical textile for the new ceiling; the chosen textile is 100% recyclable. **rp**

1 – Interior textile ceiling solution.

2 – Original concrete frame.

3 – Structural rejuvenation.

GONFREVILLE MARTIAL ARTS CENTRE AND CHESS CLUB

Location: Gonfreville-l'Orcher, France
Building type: Sports and community centre
Client: Town of Gonfreville-l'Orcher
Architects: Thierry Nabères Architectes (TNA), Paris, France
Engineer, membrane: Interlignes Déco, La Chevrolière, France
Membrane type: Open-weave polyester fibre with formulated vinyl coating and acrylic lacquer finish
Membrane area: 330 m²
Completion: 2007

The construction of a new martial arts and chess centre led to an inspired use of interior textiles. The calm, discipline and concentration required for both these pursuits are aided by the quiet intimacy brought by the hanging textile screens (1).

The centre is designed as a new "city block", dedicated to sports and relaxation, with streets, squares and delimited spaces of various size positioned between windows or walls of vegetation, defining a protected interior landscape; a neighbourhood of the future. It was decided to bring together, in the same building, two sports that have significant common traits: discipline, inner work, concentration, anticipation and respect for the opponent; thus chess and martial arts meet in a common area.

The interior textile hangings serve to absorb sound while adding light and shade during daylight hours and enhancing artificial lighting at night.

The textile chosen for this application was a vinyl-coated open-weave polyester fabric with acrylic lacquer finish. In comparison with a classic ceiling treatment this textile solution was economically viable, while its translucence and the consequential light diffusion arising from this made it the option of choice (2). In addition, the textile hangings were installed without difficulty in a period of two weeks.

A warm and exciting atmosphere is brought to this space by the lighting quality and careful attention to colours and materials (3 to 5). **rp**

1 – Quiet intimacy.

2 – Ease of installation.

3 – Light and shadow.

4 – Light diffusion: natural and artificial.

5 – Light and illumination.

KREMLIN-BICÊTRE AQUATICS CENTRE

Location: Kremlin-Bicêtre, Paris, France
Building type: Water sports centre
Client: Civic community of Val de Bièvre
Architect: Thierry Nabères Architectes (TNA), Paris
Engineer, membrane: Interlignes Déco, La Chevrolière, France

Membrane type: Open-weave polyester fibre with formulated vinyl coating and acrylic lacquer finish.
Membrane area: 2,200 m²
Completion: 2008

Tensioned textiles took on particular importance in this project. They are used in two distinct ways; in the gymnasium where wide tensioned bands of textile are placed horizontally, and over the pool where tensioned vertical textile screens are hung beneath glazed skylights to shape the overhead lighting. These vertical canopies (3) capture light from the overhead sun and, by virtue of their 50% perforation, diffuse it to both sides. This arrangement provides an excellent level of natural lighting (1).

The Kremlin-Bicêtre water sports building was constructed in the 1960s by the architects Henry-Pierre Maillard and Paul Ducamp, and inaugurated in 1969. The initial aspiration was to create a cathedral of reinforced concrete, buried between towers of urban habitation. Only the twin slopes of the swimming pool roof emerge from the ground. Due to public health concerns, the pool closed in 1999 and studies for renovating the centre began.

In the interests of sustainable development, it was decided to renovate the existing structure, giving it a new suit of clothes and exploiting renewable resources wherever possible. The preference was for materials and systems that would reduce pollution. For example the pool water is heated by geothermal energy, and the water purification relies primarily on the use of ozone sterilisation rather than chlorine.

The use of technical textile screens reinforces this initiative both by improving the ambient lighting and by being 100% recyclable. The textile chosen for this application was a vinyl-coated open-weave polyester fabric with an acrylic lacquer finish.

The textile screens are hung from metal anchorage rails and tensioned below by weighting rods inserted in the hem along the lower screen edge. Installation was thus relatively straightforward (2).

Concerning the acoustic properties, particular attention was paid to selecting materials that would absorb the echoes typically experienced in such structures. In this respect the textile screens played an important role. The appropriate choice of materials and colours was essential for lighting and for the acoustics of the large volumes. All were opportunities to reveal the building's architectural qualities.

One of the major goals in architecture is to achieve the desired level of lighting. The imaginative use of technical textiles in this renovation has, by relatively simple means, enhanced the natural internal lighting and improved the centre's acoustic qualities. In the pool area, light diffusion is aided by reflection from the water surface and from the surrounding walls.

A warm and exciting atmosphere is brought to this space by the lighting quality and careful attention to colours and materials (4). **rp**

1 – Enhanced natural lighting.

2 – Illuminating the renovated pool.

3 – Solar protection and diffusion.

4 – Swimming in light.

VHV GROUP HEAD-QUARTERS

Location: Hanover, Germany
Building type: Three linked multi-storey buildings around an atrium
Client: Hannoversche Lebensversicherung AG
Architects: Architekten BKSP Grabau Leiber Obermann und Partner, Hanover
General Contractor: Investa Projektentwicklungs- und Verwaltungs GmbH, Munich, Germany

Membrane engineering and installation: Ellermann GmbH, Rietberg, Germany
Membrane type: Fibreglass substrate with formulated vinyl coating
Membrane area: Elevators 650 m², stairwell approx. 300 m²
Completion: 2009

Due to strong growth in the past, the VHV insurance group's headquarters in Hanover were spread over three locations in the town. The purpose of the new headquarters was, in terms of organisation and communication, to regroup and enhance working practices of the over 2,000 employees while creating a state-of-the-art energy concept.

The new headquarters were designed as three linked, but independent buildings and connected by a striking atrium. The atrium symbolises the open and transparent character of the building and forms the central access area and intersection (1).

The architectural focal point within the atrium is the impressive twin elevator tower, which is responsible for transport to the six or seven storeys of the linked buildings. The idea behind the twin elevator towers was to lend the atrium "support" in terms of proportions and to create a particular highlight at night thanks to a special light installation (2).

During the tendering phase, a company specialising in textile architecture and concepts scored highly with its detailed planning and suggestions for textiles.

A high-tech textile was presented that fulfilled the architects' demands in their entirety. In addition to a high level of translucence and the certified noise-reduction effect to minimise echo in the voluminous atrium, the special fibreglass membrane also exceeded fire protection regulations. Its A2 classification (non-flammable) in line with DIN 4102, gives an additional level of safety for this much-frequented building (6).

The design of the two membrane tubes includes an upper steel support ring, installed as part of the initial elevator construction, with a series of aluminium rings suspended from it (5). These are mounted directly onto wire cables and fixed in position at the base by a supporting ring that allows overall adjustment of the tube height with regard to that of the structure. This was a vital condition in order to compensate for movements caused by thermal expansion, resulting from building settlement, and from forces generated by elevator motion.

In order to ensure a perfectly smooth surface for the textile tube segments, while taking account of flexure and shaft tolerances, the membrane designer created a special fixing detail. The aluminium keder profile provides the socket for the special elastic keder strip, which is fastened to the membrane textile. The elasticity allows for the relaxation of any residual tensions that would otherwise be transferred to the membrane; the fibreglass textile has material characteristics that render it fairly stiff and hence unable to absorb elongations.

A secondary focal point is provided by the atrium's stairwell, which is partially screened by a similar membrane structure designed to match the appearance of the elevator towers (3). The membrane solution's light weight enabled maximum allocation of the available stairwell width to pedestrian traffic; the membrane screen is fixed to metal profiles that wrap around 330 mm diameter support columns to occupy only 600 mm of the available width. Precise laser cutting of the metal profiles allowed close construction tolerances to be met (4). **rp and ws**

1 – The transparent atrium linking three independent building blocks.

2 – Illuminated elevator towers provide the focal point.

3 – The matching stairwell-screen cladding.

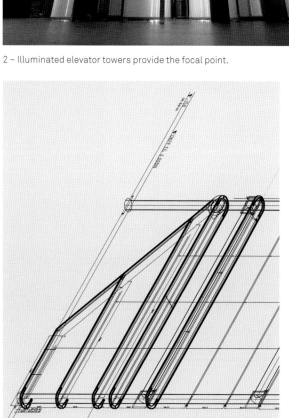

4 – The stairwell cladding's laser-cut fastening profiles.

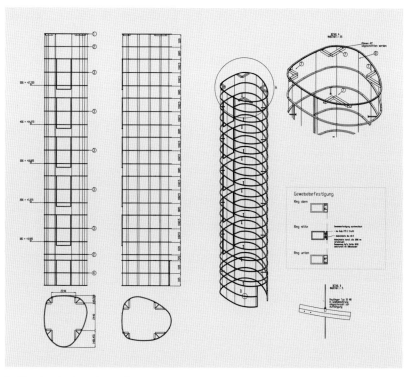

5 – The elevator tower's membrane support structure.

6 – The membrane, fixed to aluminium rings, minimises echo and is non-flammable.

BIBLIOGRAPHY

Architen-Landrell. "The materials of tensile architecture". http://www.architen.com.

Barnes, M.R. "Applications of dynamic relaxation to the design and analysis of cable, membrane and pneumatic structures". In: *Proceedings of the 2nd International Conference on Space Structures*. New York: Guildford, 1975.

Bletzinger, K.U.; Ramm, E. "A general finite element approach to the form finding of tensile structures by the updated reference strategy". *International Journal of Space Structures*, vol. 14, 1999, p. 131–246.

Blum, R. "Acoustics and heat transfer in textile architecture". Lecture presented at Techtextil. Frankfurt am Main, 2003.

Braddock Clarke, S.E.; O'Mahony, M. *Techno textiles 2: Revolutionary fabrics for fashion and design*. London: Thames and Hudson, 2008.

Breuer, J.; Ockels, W.; Luchsinger, R.H. "An inflatable wing using the principle of Tensairity". In: *Proceedings of the 48th AIAA/ASME/ASCE/AHS/ASC Structures, Structural Dynamics and Materials Conference*. Hawaii, 2007.

Cox, M.D.G.M.; Gijsbers, R.; Haas, T.C.A. "Applied design of an energy-efficient multi-layered membrane roofing system for climate-control of semi-permanent shelters". In: Kenny, P. et al. (ed.). *Proceedings of the 25th PLEA International Conference on Passive and Low Energy Architecture, 22nd–24th October 2008*. University College Dublin, 2008.

Doriez, B. (ed.). *Architecture textile*. Paris: Éditions A Tempera, 1990.

Drew, P. *Structures tendues, une architecture nouvelle*. Paris: Éditions Actes Sud, 2008.

Forster, B.; Mollaert, M. *European design guide for tensile surface structures*. Brussels: Tensinet, 2004.

Galliot, C.; Luchsinger, R.H. "A simple model describing the non-linear biaxial tensile behavior of PVC-coated polyester fabrics for use in finite ele-

ment analysis". *Composite Structures* 90 (4) (2009). P. 438–447.

Haas, T.C.A. de. *Boogstal voor de varkenshouderij*. Graduation report, Eindhoven University of Technology. Eindhoven, 2008.

Haber, R.B.; Abel, J. F. "Initial equilibrium solution methods for cable reinforced membranes – Part I and II". *Computer Methods in Applied Mechanics and Engineering* 30, 1982, p. 263–89 and p. 285–306.

Haug, E.; Powell, G.H. "Finite element analysis of nonlinear membrane structures". In: *IASS Pacific Symposium on Tension Structures and Space Frames*. Tokyo and Kyoto, 1972, p. 124–135.

Herzog, T.; Minke, G.; Eggers, H. *Pneumatische Konstruktionen*. Stuttgart: Hatje Cantz Verlag, 1976.

Humphries, M. *Fabric reference*. Fourth edition. Saddle River, NJ: Pearson Education Incorporated, 2009.

International Association for Shell and Spatial Structures (ed.). *Recommendations for air-supported structures*. IASS Working group on pneumatic structures. Madrid, 1985.

Ishii, K. *Membrane designs and structures in the world*. Tokyo: Shinkenchiku-sha, 1995.

Knoll, W.H.; Wagenaar, E. J.; van Weele, A.M. *Handboek installatietechniek*. Rotterdam: Stichting ISSO, 2002.

De Laet, L.; Luchsinger, R.H.; Crettol, R.; Mollaert. M.; De Temmermann, N. "Deployable tensairity structures". *Journal of the International Association for Shell and Spatial Structures* 50(2), 2009, p. 121–128.

Linkwitz, K.; Schek, H.-J. "Einige Bemerkungen zur Berechnung von vorgespannten Seilnetzkonstruktionen". *Ingenieur-Archiv* 40, 1971, p. 145-158.

Luchsinger, R.H.; Pedretti, A.; Steingruber, P.; Pedretti, M. "Lightweight structures with Tensairity". In: Motro, R. (ed.), *Shell and Spatial Structures from Models to Realizations*. Montpellier: Éditions de l'Espérou, 2004.

Luchsinger, R.H.; Pedretti, A.; Steingruber, P.; Pedretti, M. "The new structural concept Tensairity: Basic principles". In: Zingoni, A. (ed.), *Progress in Structural Engineering, Mechanics and Computations*. London: Balkema, 2004.

Luchsinger, R.H.; Crettol, R. "Experimental and numerical study of spindle shaped Tensairity girders". *International Journal of Space Structures* 21 (3), 2006, p. 119–130.

Luchsinger, R.H.; Crettol, R.; Plagianakos, T.S. "Temporary structures with Tensairity". *International Symposium IASS-SLTE 2008, 3rd Latin American Symposium on Tensile Structures*. Acapulco, 2008.

Lyonnet, C. "Les structures textiles tendues. Analyse de l'existant et identification des problèmes posés". *Cahiers du CSTB* 336, issue 2633 (January/February 1993).

Meffert, B. "Mechanische Eigenschaften PVC-beschichteter Polyestergewebe". Doctoral thesis, RWTH Aachen. Aachen, 1978.

Membrane Structures Association of Japan (ed.), *Testing method for elastic constants of membrane materials*. MSAJ/M-02, 1995.

Motro, R.; Maurin, B. *Membranes textiles architecturales. Comportement mécanique des systèmes tissés*. London: Hermès Science Publishing/Cachan: Lavoisier, 2006, p. 17–70.

Otto, F.; Trostel, R. *Zugbeanspruchte Konstruktionen*. Frankfurt am Main: Ullstein Fachverlag, 1962.

Otto, F.; Trostel, R. *Tensile structures*. Vol. 2. Cambridge, MA: MIT Press, 1967.

Otto, F. *Tensile structures*. Vols. 1 and 2. Cambridge, MA: MIT Press, 1973.

Pedretti, M.; Luscher, R. "Tensairity-Patent – Eine pneumatische Tenso-Struktur". *Stahlbau* 76 (5), 2007, p. 314–319.

Pedretti, A.; Steingruber, P.; Pedretti, M.; Luchsinger, R.H. "The new struc-

tural concept Tensairity: FE-modeling and applications". Zingoni, A. (ed.), *Progress in Structural Engineering, Mechanics and Computations*. London: Balkema, 2004.

Plagianakos, T.S.; Teutsch, U.; Crettol, R.; Luchsinger, R.H. "Static response of a spindle-shaped Tensairity column to axial compression". *Engineering Structures* 31, 2009, p. 1822–1831.

Pronk, A.D.C.; Haas, T.C.A. de; Cox, M.G.D.M. "Heat-adapting membrane". In: *Proceedings of the Structural Membranes Conference*. Barcelona, 2007.

Quinn, B. *Textile Futures: Fashion, Design and Technology*. New York: Berg Publishing, 2010.

Ritter, A. *Smart materials in architecture, interior architecture and design*. Basel, Berlin, Boston: Birkhäuser Verlag, 2007.

Rowe, T. (ed.). *Interior Textiles – Design and Developments*. Oxford: Woodhead Publishing, 2009.

Santomauro, R. *Tensoestructuras*. Montevideo: Mastergraf, 2008.

Schock, H.-J. *Soft shells. Design and technology of tensile architecture*. Basel, Berlin, Boston: Birkhäuser Verlag, 1997, p. 102–105.

Teutsch, U. *Tragverhalten von Tensairity-Trägern*. Zurich: vdf Hochschulverlag, 2011.

Topham, S. *Blow up: inflatable art, architecture and design*. Munich: Prestel Verlag, 2002.

Wakefield, W.; Bown, A. "Marsyas, a large fabric scultpure: construction engineering and installation". In: Onate, E.; Köplin, B. (ed.), *Proceedings of Textile Composite Deflatable Structures Conference*. Barcelona: CIMNE, 2003.

Acknowledgements

After many years of fruitful cooperation between Serge Ferrari group and the research team "Structures Design" (Laboratory for Mechanics and Civil Engineering, University of Montpellier 2), Françoise Fournier, in charge of textile architecture in the group, suggested that I could act as editor for a book devoted to "Flexible Composite Materials in Architecture, Construction and Interiors". Since I did not know that it was an almost impossible task, I accepted the challenge! It is my personal pleasure to warmly thank Françoise Fournier for her proposal; she never appears to the foreground, but without her discreet action, nothing would be possible. That is why I am anxious to grant her symbolically the first place in these acknowledgements. As researcher I have always had the support of Sébastien Ferrari and Romain Ferrari. Could they find in these words the expression of my gratitude!

It is a matter of fact that a close collaboration with the editors is a key point. I want to express my most sincere thanks to the editors who combined their experience, their patience, their attention to each and every detail so as to produce and realise this book. After my first meetings with Andreas Müller, I worked mainly with Henriette Mueller-Stahl, helped by Michael Wachholz during some months. I learned a lot with them on this demanding job, and I learned also from the assistance of Richard Palmer who acted very actively for the third part of the book.

During this work I had the chance to meet some people who contributed to thread links to find the appropriate contacts, who answered a need. I wish that they know that I am grateful to them for it. Among them trying not to forget someone I want to quote John Chilton, Manfred Grohmann, Harald Kloft, Kazuo Ishii, Nicolas Pauli, Ronald Shaeffer, Ali Smaili, Jean Vasseur, Bell Warwick and Qiling Zhang.

This publication would not have been possible without the cooperation of all authors, of all the architects and engineers and whose projects are presented and numerous photographers who have documented the case studies. I do hope that nobody has been forgotten in the texts for their active contribution. Among them I had to work more closely with Thomas Becksmann, Stefano Bertino, Christian Blaser, Bernard Doriez, Nicolas Goldsmith, Rolf H. Luchsinger, Andrea Giovanni Mainini, Bernard Maurin, Thierry Nabères, Tiziana Poli, Arno Pronk, Walter D. Runza, Osama Thawadi, Ivo Vrouwe and Liliane Wong.

Last, but not least, I want to thank all those who share my life, either on the professional part or private one. They will recognise themselves.

ABOUT THE AUTHORS

Stefano Bertino, born in 1957 in Bergamo (Italy), studied architecture at the Polytechnic Institute of Milan (1983). He has been fascinated by lightweight structures ever since his graduation, exploring their architectural potential in a constant crossover of skills, ideas, tools and technologies. He is the founder of the company Tensoforma Trading Srl in Italy. For many years he collaborated with AIC Architekten+Ingenieure of Stuttgart and worked as a tutor at the European Institute of Design (IED) in Milan. His work and research focus on lightweight structures, textile architecture and architectural applications of textile techniques; he has also patented several products and fabrication processes.

Mark Cox, born in 1968 in Roermond (The Netherlands), studied physics at Eindhoven University of Technology, from which he graduated in1995. He worked for several years in the industry as a consultant for building physics, building services and architectural product development. Since 2005 he has been working as a researcher in the Department of Architecture, Building and Planning at Eindhoven University of Technology. Most of his current research is done in cooperation with Roel Gijsbers, a doctoral researcher on flexible structures, and Tim de Haas. Their research is focused on the development of new products and concepts for the improvement of flexibility, comfort and energy efficiency, and geared towards various smaller and mid-sized companies that cooperate with academic researchers for technological innovation.

Bernard Doriez, born in 1952 in Arras (France), founded the company SNBBS in Sète in 1982. From 1990 to 1995 he was vice-president of the Architecture Textile Commission at Relais des Textiles Techniques, a European network with members in ten countries. He is the editor of the book Architecture Textile (Éditions A Tempera) and was the organizer of the conference "Rencontres de l'architecture textile" at Nîmes in 1990. Today, he works as a consultant and technical expert associated with Relais des Textiles Techniques and Serge Ferrari.

Romain Ferrari was born in Lyon in 1960. After graduating from high school with a concentration in the sciences, he studied for the entrance examination of the Hydrography School of the merchant navy, which he joined in 1980. He obtained in 1983 his Polyvalent Officer diploma in civil and industrial engineering (C1NM degree) and became a first class captain in sea navigation. Mobilised as a reserve officer of the navy, he served between 1984 and 1985 in Lebanon on the Clémenceau aircraft carrier. After working for five years as a project engineer for the enginering company TECHNIP, he set up his own business. He has been managing director of the firm Ferrari Textiles, now Serge Ferrari, since 1991. Romain Ferrari is also a member of the association Terre démocrate (Democratic Earth), for which he has conducted a workshop on eco-friendly production technologies. This association is committed to the implementation of the values of ecology, democracy and humanism in the economic realm. Romain Ferrari has also created Fondation 2019, a research foundation promoting studies in environmental economics.

Roel Gijsbers, born 1981 in Boekel (The Netherlands), works as a researcher in building technology and product development at the Department of the Built Environment at Eindhoven University of Technology. He developed the flexible arched shed system Boogstal and co-developed a number of spin-off projects. His dissertation dealt with flexible use and adaptability of buildings, with a special focus on structural adaptability. Other research activities are focused on post-disaster shelter solutions.

Ines de Giuli, born in 1981, is an historian and art historian. She specialised in cultural history and worked on the artistic relationship between the painters of the post-World War Two School of Paris and Japan, where she lived for two years. She has written a local history book commissioned by the town of Vaucresson near Paris, and was a project manager for the art collection of the French bank Société Générale. She joined the team of Histoire d'Entreprises in 2010 (www.histoire-entreprises.fr).

Tim de Haas, born in 1980 in Geleen (The Netherlands), studied building technology in Haarlem and architectural product development at Eindhoven University of Technology (2008). He wrote his thesis on a tensile heat recovery unit as a part of a translucent tensile roof. Since 2007 he has been researcher in the Department of Architecture, Building and Planning at Eindhoven University of Technology, working in a variety of fields such as building physics, building technology, structural engineering, product development and post-disaster sheltering. In particular, his research concentrates on the development of new products and concepts for small and medium enterprises and non-governmental organisations, focusing on increased flexibility, comfort and energy efficiency.

Rolf H. Luchsinger, born in 1966 in Aarau (Switzerland), holds a Ph.D. in computational physics. After several years of scientific research in academia and industry, he joined the Swiss company Prospective Concepts AG in 2002, where he specialised in fabric structures and inflatable structures. Since 2006 he has been heading the Center for Synergetic Structures at Empa, the Swiss Federal Laboratories for Materials Science and Technologies, with a major focus in the R&D of new lightweight structures, in particular the Tensairity technology. He is the author of numerous scientific publications.

Andrea Giovanni Mainini, born in 1980 in Gallarate (Italy), holds a Ph.D. in building engineering from the Polytechnic Institute of Milan. Currently he is a post-doctoral fellow in building technology and energy simulation. He is a member of the TiSco Group at the Department of Building Environment Science and Technology (B.E.S.T.) at the Polytechnic Institute of Milan. His research focuses on energy efficiency of buildings, zero-energy houses and the use of renewable resources, innovation of building envelope products, thermal-bridge optimisation, optical and solar characterisation of building skins. He has also worked as an energy consultant for the building product industry, and has taught professional development courses on energy certification. He is

the author of numerous national and some international publications.

Bernard Maurin is professor at the University of Montpellier 2 where he heads the Conceptual Design in Structures team of the Mechanical and Civil Engineering Laboratory. His research interests are directed towards the form-finding and conceptual design of innovative structures: lightweight structures (tensile membranes and thin concrete shells), tensegrity systems (non-regular shapes, grids and rings), lightweight hybrid deployable structures (space applications), free-form architecture (parametrics, Pascalian forms "pForms") and structural morphology (structuration, emergence, self-organisation).

Anais Missakian, born in Geneva, is a professor at the Rhode Island School of Design's Textile Department where she also serves as department head. A design consultant for the textile industry, she has spent the last 25 years designing textile collections for the interior market. Anais Missakian received her Bachelor of Fine Arts in textiles at RISD after attending Michigan State University and Central Saint Martins College of Art and Design in London.

René Motro, born in 1946 in Paris, devoted his scientific work to lightweight structures: space structures, tensegrity systems, structural morphology and textile architecture. He published in numerous international journals, delivered papers at more than 150 conferences, wrote and/or co-edited five books and participated in many collective publications. Emeritus Professor at the University of Montpellier, he is editor-in-chief of the International Journal of Space Structures and president of the International Association for Shell and Spatial Structures (IASS). He received the Tsuboi Award three times (1998, 2007 and 2009) and the Pioneer Award in 2002.

Khipra Nichols, born in Pennsylvania, is an associate professor and director of the Master's program in industrial design at the Rhode Island School of Design. He received his Bachelor in industrial design from RISD, and before joining the faculty full-time in 1998, Khipra Nichols was a design director at Hasbro's Playskool Baby Division. During his career at Hasbro, he was awarded 16 U.S. patents in infant, toy and juvenile product design, and over 250 of his designs have entered the marketplace.

Richard Palmer, born in 1955 in Reading (England), studied civil engineering at the University of Manchester, becoming a chartered engineer practicing in the UK and worldwide. Today he specialises in the performance and preservation of buildings and civil engineering structures, working from his base in Southeast France near Lac Léman. A passion for technology and the written word led him to writing and editing technical publications.

Tiziana Poli, born in 1968 in Milan, holds a Ph.D. in building engineering and is an associate professor in architecture and building technology at the Polytechnic Institute of Milan. Since 2003, she has been a member of the scientific committee of the Built Environment Science and Technology Laboratory (B.E.S.T.) at the same institute. Her research is focused on building envelope performances and technologies for low-energy buildings; the optical and solar characterisation of building skins; the innovation of building envelope's products, components and systems; the mitigation of urban heat island effects and the effects of building skins on the urban micro-climate. She has also worked as a consultant for the building and engineering industries, and is the author of numerous national and international publications.

Arno Pronk, born in 1967 in Anna Jacobapolder (The Netherlands), studied architecture at Delft University of Technology. After his graduation in 1994, he worked as an architectural product developer and architect, invented several patented products and was an assistant professor at Delft University of Technology. His current positions: assistant professor for product development at Eindhoven University of Technology, lecturer and research coordinator for building technology at the School of Architecture Sint-Lucas/LUCA (a partner in the KU Leuven Association), chief editor of *NBD-bouwdetails* and co-president

of the International Society of Fabric Forming (ISOFF). The main focus of his research is on flexible moulding techniques in relation to fluid architecture.

Wolfgang Sterz, born in 1964 in Landshut (Germany), qualified as a business manager in media production at the Technical College for Publishing in Munich. He then embarked on his career as a layout editor and production manager for the architectural magazine *AIT*. Over the years he has focused increasingly on advertising and business communication. Since 1997 he has been co-owner of the advertising and PR agency HTP Communications in Munich. In his role as a consultant, PR manager and author of project documentations, he works for international clients, primarily from the construction, architecture and interior design sector.

Jean Vasseur, born in 1964, is a former radio journalist working in France and the United States. He launched his first business, Jean Vasseur Communication, in 1990. Since then, he has created several companies and established a mid-size communication group that offers a full range of services, including digital and interactive communication. Most recently, he founded the first magazine devoted to business history in France, Histoire d'Entreprises (www.histoire-entreprises.fr).

Ivo Vrouwe, born in 1979 in Amsterdam, studied building technology in Amsterdam and architectural product development at Eindhoven University of Technology (2006). He worked as a technical designer and engineer of membrane structures at Tentech in Utrecht and as a tutor at Eindhoven University of Technology. In 2008 he started his own practice, Workshop IV, as an architectural designer and engineer. He lectures at the Utrecht School of the Arts and the School of Architecture Sint-Lucas/LUCA (a partner in the KU Leuven Association). His research and work are focused on artistic and architectural applications of textile techniques and tectonics.

Liliane Wong, born in Hong Kong, earned a Master of Architecture from Harvard University, Graduate School of Design, and a B.A. in mathematics

from Vassar College. She is a professor at the Rhode Island School of Design where she has taught since 1998. She currently heads the Department of Interior Architecture. She is the co-founder and co-editor of the *Int|AR Journal on Interventions and Adaptive Reuse*. Liliane Wong is also a registered architect in the state of Massachusetts.

Jeroen Weijers, born in 1984 in Roermond (The Netherlands), studied building technology and architectural product development at Eindhoven University of Technology (2010). Since his graduation with a thesis on a prefabricated component as part of a smart solar housing renovation concept, he has worked as a façade engineer. Focusing on sustainable low-energy building envelopes, he integrates product engineering and innovation in challenging architectural designs.

INDEX

ILLUSTRATION CREDITS

Chapter 1:
P. 8, 10, 12, 14, 18, 20, 21, 22, 25 ©Serge Ferrari; p. 16 Sto AG; p. 23 Schmidhuber & Kaindl, Munich

Chapters 2 to 7:
2.1–2.4 Nicolas Pauli; 2.5, 2.6 Bernard Maurin; 2.7, 2.8 René Motro; 2.9 Bernard Maurin; 2.10 René Motro; 2.11 ILEK Stuttgart; 2.12. Bernard Maurin; 2.13 Bernard Maurin, ILEK Stuttgart; 2.14 René Motro; 2.15 Bernard Maurin; 2.16, 2.17 Nicolas Pauli

3.1–3.11 Bernard Doriez; 3.12 René Motro; 3.13, 3.14 Bernard Doriez; 3.15 Nicolas Pauli; 3.16–3.27 Bernard Doriez

4.1, 4.2 Tensoforma Trading Srl – TEXO® system; 4.3 SMIT; 4.4 Tensoforma Trading Srl – TEXO® system; 4.5 DuPont; 4.6–4.9 Tensoforma Trading Srl – TEXO® system; 4.10 Planungsgruppe Drahtler – Dortmund, Tensoforma Trading Srl – TEXO® system; 4.11– 4.13 Tensoforma Trading Srl – TEXO® system; 4.14 Archea Associati; 4.15 Tensoforma Trading Srl – TEXO® system

5.1–5.18 Mark Cox, Tim de Haas, Roel Gijsbers, Arno Pronk, Jeroen Weijers

6.1 Jouve-Sazerat-Vignaud Architects, Sophie Mallebranche; 6.2 Wikimedia Commons; 6.3 Anna Zaharakos, Studio Z; 6.4 Anne Kyyrö Quinn; 6.5 Camilla Diedrich; 6.6. Davide Giordano – Zaha Hadid Architects; 6.7 Giuseppe Crispino, Antonio Ravalli Architetti; 6.8, 6.9 Sophie Smith – Wil Alsop; 6.10 INFLATE Design; 6.11 Kurt Tingdal, Offecct AB; 6.12 Paul Kaloustian; 6.13 Anne Kyyro Quinn; 6.14 Hsinming Fung, Architect and Craig Hodgetts, Architect; 6.15 Paúl Rivera/Arch Photo; 6.16 Architen Landrell; 6.17 Wikimedia Commons; 6.18 Annette Kisling/Cy Twombly, 2009; 6.19 Ricardo Santonja/Alberto Cubas; 6.20 Marcel Wanders; 6.21, 6.22 Erwan & Ronan Bouroullec; 6.23 Werner Aisslinger/studio Aisslinger; 6.24 Astrid Krogh; 6.25 Cristiano Peruzzi, Luminex®; 6.26 Camilla Diedrich; 6.27 Erin Hayne, Nuno Erin; 6.28 Mette Ramsgard Thomsen; 6.29 Future Shape GmbH; 6.30 Wikimedia Commons.

7.1–7.22 Empa – Center for Synergetic Structures

Chapters 8 to 11:

P. 115–117 Esmery Caron
P. 119–121 Esmery Caron
P. 123–125 WAGG Soluciones Tensadas
P. 127 Ali Smaili, Smaili Contracting
P. 129–133 Tourism New Zealand (1 top), Cameron Spencer, Getty Images (1 bottom), Fabric Structure Systems (3, 5, 7), ©Spyglass Group Ltd. (6, 9)
P. 135–137 ©Serge Ferrari
P. 139–143 Lonas Lorenzo, Roberto Munoz
P. 145–149 Tentech
P. 151–153 Prat Structures Avancées
P. 157–159 Lilli Kehl (1,3); Archiv Blaser Architekten AG (2, 4, 5)
P. 161–165 Photos: Marc Blessano, drawings: deillon delley architectes
P. 171–175 Architecture: Schmidhuber & Kaindl/Exhibition: Milla + Partner/ Photos: Andreas Keller
P. 177 ©Serge Ferrari, photographer: Marco Blessano
P. 179–183 Iaso
P. 186–191 Gulf Shade, Manama, Bahrain
P. 193–195 Ali Smaili, Ali Smaili Contracting
P. 197–199 Thomas Mayer archive
P. 201–203 ©Serge Ferrari, photographer: Marco Blessano
P. 205–207 Gilles Aymard
P. 211–213 Paul Kozlowski (1, 3, 4, 5), TNA (2)
P. 215–217 Paul Kozlowski (1, 3, 4, 5), TNA (2)
P. 219–223 Paul Kozlowski (1, 3, 4,), TNA (2)
P. 225–227 Ellermann GmbH; Fria Hagen